A Walking Guide to
North Carolina's
Historic
New Bern

A WALKING GUIDE *TO* NORTH CAROLINA'S HISTORIC

New Bern

Bill Hand

RECOMMENDED BY THE NEW BERN HISTORICAL SOCIETY

THE
History
PRESS

Published by The History Press
Charleston, SC 29403
www.historypress.net

Cover image: Watercolor of the Stanley House, by Janet Francoeur.

All images courtesy of the author unless otherwise noted.

First published 2007
Second printing 2014

Manufactured in the United States

ISBN 978.1.59629.272.7

Library of Congress Cataloging-in-Publication Data

Hand, Bill, 1956-
A walking guide to North Carolina's historic New Bern / Bill Hand.
p. cm.
ISBN-13: 978-1-59629-272-7 (alk. paper) 1. New Bern (N.C.)--Tours. 2. Historic
buildings--North Carolina--New Bern--Guidebooks. 3. Historic sites--North Carolina-
-New Bern--Guidebooks.
4. New Bern (N.C.)--Buildings, structures, etc.--Guidebooks. 5.
Walking--North Carolina--New Bern--Guidebooks. 6. New Bern (N.C.)--History.
I. Title.
F264.N5H36 2007
917.56'192--dc22
2007015733

To Roberta
Twenty-five years and still loving you

Contents

Acknowledgements

Thanks to all involved, but especially:

First and foremost Dick Lore, New Bern historian extraordinaire. He gave a lot of fine suggestions and read over this work with a fine eye. Also to John Green and the rest of the staff at the Craven Regional Library's excellent Kellenberger Room—

Morning dew forms on reeds along the Neuse River.

and to Dean Knight and Nancy Richards of Tryon Palace. Many homeowners were helpful as well. Thanks to them all!

On the homefront, to Roberta, who supports and tolerates my obsessions with history, and to my daughters, Rachel and Sara, who likewise don't seem to mind.

I'd especially like to thank the Newsom Williams and the New Bern Historical Society for their support and encouragement on this project.

I owe endless kudos to Peter B. Sandbeck's *Historic Architecture of New Bern and Craven County, North Carolina*. If you wish to learn more about these houses please turn to this fine volume.

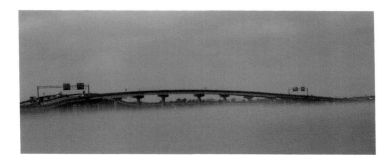

The Neuse River Bridge spans a one-and-a-half-mile stretch of water and morning mist. It is one of three vital bridges connecting New Bern to surrounding towns.

Lee Handford of The History Press has been endlessly fruitful for me, as have the other editors and staff there.

Also, significant portions of research were taken from two nineteenth-century manuscripts, Stephen F. Miller's *Recollections of New Bern Fifty Years Ago* (written in 1875) and Colonel John D. Whitford's jumbled but fascinating *The Home Story of a Walking Stick*.

About These Tours

I want you to see how these houses fit in—as footprints of our past. Our focus is on who lived there. How did they affect our history? What were they like? How do they define who we've become?

I present to you four tours. In each you will examine ten houses or other buildings (the church tour features nine). In some cases, you will walk several blocks between houses, but that's okay—there are some beautiful homes not covered in this tour. The length of the tour depends on you—from an hour to a day, if you take time to tour available homes, admire additional buildings and shop.

Grab your walking stick and enjoy.

New Bern is a moving town—moving houses, among other things. The Stanly House was moved from Middle and New Streets to George Street in 1966. *Courtesy of Tryon Palace Historic Sites and Gardens.*

FOR STARTERS, LET'S MEET THE BEARS...

We hope you like bears. A gigantic painting of one greets you when you come into town on Highway 70, from east or west. Once here, you will see them everywhere: painted on the government vehicles, silhouetted on shields, wooden sculptures guarding the gift shops or populating little parks, even coming through the second-story walls of the quaint city hall.

Blame it on Duke Berthold V and his redneck ways. A Switzer with a penchant for big game, he founded a city in 1191 and named it after a bear he had killed—or so we are told. The Bernians

adopted the bear as their symbol (a rather thirsty bear, to judge by his long, curling tongue) and New Bern, official sister city to that European center of commerce, has followed suit with abundant bruins of our own.

WILDLIFE

New Bern is not Atlantic City. The party life and Elvis look-alikes aren't here. Our wildlife is of a more genteel nature. Foxes are often seen at night and owls haunt the building façades. We have that fine old charmer, the mockingbird, and being a river, fowl are plenteous. And don't forget those ever-inquisitive hucksters, the squirrels…

Union Point Park in downtown New Bern is always a good place to find water birds such as these mallards, gulls and coots.

Above: A mockingbird sings at Cedar Grove cemetery.

Right: Jester of the city, a squirrel plays by a light post.

Below: Pigeons huddle in the winter sun at the Shriner's Sudan Temple.

Colonial–Antebellum Walking Tour

FOUNDING FATHERS

At first we were Chatooka, the residence of a small tribe of Neusioc, relatives of the fierce Tuscarora. They lived here at the confluence of the Neuse and Trent Rivers, having little intercourse with Europeans other than a curious surveyor with a love of plants: John Lawson.

Mr. Lawson had crossed the Atlantic from London in 1700, seeking adventure in a new land. He arrived in Charleston at a time when the two Carolinas were ruled by five Lords Proprietors instead of one king. These gentlemen asked Lawson to explore the Carolinas and he did so, setting out on a chilly December day in 1770 with five Englishmen and four Indians in a canoe up the Santee River.

They sailed northwest toward the present North Carolina border, then veered

The C.J. Sauthier map of New Bern, drawn 1769. Note the old racetrack, close to where Queen Street runs today. *Courtesy of Tryon Palace Historic Sites and Gardens.*

east and ended their travels near Pamlico. He found time, in 1705, to lay out our oldest town, Bath, and also set up a home on Lawson Creek in what is now New Bern proper. It was a fine place, he believed, if one could overlook the alligator nesting beneath his house. He wrote a book (*A New Voyage to Carolina*) and, in 1709, sailed to London to see it printed.

There he met Franz Michel, a Swiss who was seeking a place to found a colony of Swiss men. Lawson sold him on "the land between two rivers," and the two then approached another Switzer who happened to be in town—Baron Christopher von Graffenried.

Graffenried was a nobleman with a habit of living above his means, and at this time he was particularly seeking to find a way to improve his financial lot. It didn't take long for Michel and Lawson to sell him on funding the new colony, which he imagined would soon be awash with silver mines. Graffenried purchased several thousand acres from the Lords Proprietors and set about selecting his new colonists—a mixture of Swiss citizens and Palatine refugees. These latter, former residents along the Rhine, were living in England as refugees from taxes, failed crops and Catholic persecutions.

The Palatines (with Lawson and Michel) arrived in New Bern in March; Graffenried arrived with the Swiss colonists in the fall of the same year, setting New Bern's birthday at 1710.

It was no easy delivery. Half or more of the Palatines had died in the passage, and they were to the point of starving shortly after their arrival here. Graffenried was outraged at their condition. He purchased more supplies (on a loan from Thomas Pollock, one of the wealthiest men in the colony) and, over the course of winter and spring of 1711, the colony turned around—only to be undone by greed and politics.

The local Tuscarora were growing angry: the Europeans—Graffenried's settlers as well as English settlers such as William Brice who had preceded them into the area—had been cheating them and, worse, kidnapping their women and children to sell into slavery. Now, they believed, the time was ripe for revenge.

Meanwhile, a small-scale civil war among the colonists (over who was the rightful governor) had resulted in bloodshed and political chaos. Disease was rampant, crops were failing and the militia—if one had the imagination to call it that—was under armed, under trained and ill led. What better time, the Tuscarora concluded, to launch a surprise war?

John Lawson—ironically, an admirer and defender of their race—was the first victim. He and Graffenried had begun a canoe trip up the Neuse on September 10, 1711, to explore the region, and stumbled onto the principle Indian village of Catechna, where the tribes were planning their war. In part due to the threats of Governor Spotswood of Virginia, Graffenried survived; Lawson, however, after arguing with a chief, was executed, possibly by torture.

On September 22, the Tuscarora and their allies swept through the region, killing 140 men, women and children. Homes, livestock, barns and crops were swept away with their owners. The Indians promised their hostage, Graffenried, that New Bern itself would be spared—but most of his settlers actually lived outside the town.

A hastily formed North Carolina militia made a few attempts at fighting in that war, but mostly they did themselves no honor; William Brice only worsened things when he captured an unoffending Indian chief and roasted him alive.

In the end, with the help of South Carolina Indians and militia, the Tuscarora were defeated and driven away. But New Bern was only a remainder of itself; Graffenried, hopelessly bankrupt from trying to keep the young colony alive, mortgaged everything to Thomas Pollock and returned to Europe, where he would write an extensive defense of his stay, laying all the settlement's faults and failures on Lawson and the English. Most of the Palatines and Switzers he left lost the land they'd been promised to Mr. Pollock, who became the largest landholder in what was left of the town.

COLONIAL CAPITAL

Tryon Palace is a recreation of the original palace, designed and built by John Hawks for Governor William Tryon in 1767–70. The palace is built on its original foundations and is open to the public. A fee is charged.

Over the ensuing years New Bern slowly regained its footing, developing an important seaport trade that would not disappear until the twentieth century. In 1729, four of the five Lords Proprietors sold their interests in the colony to the king, and North Carolina officially became a Crown colony.

For a time, the Albermarle region—especially Edenton—was the center of government. But New Bern quickly outpaced her neighbors in size and influence. The town hosted its first general assembly in 1737 under Governor Gabriel Johnson. To hold down territorial animosities, the governors began rotating assembly meetings between the principal towns of Edenton, New Bern and Wilmington. This maintained a balance of power, but caused an obvious strain on the vital records, which were constantly being transported from town to town.

Johnson convinced the assembly to name New Bern the official capital in 1747. It scored again two years later when James Davis arrived from Williamsburg and set up the colony's first printing press. Among his first publications was a revision of North Carolina's laws. Soon he was churning out the weekly *North Carolina Gazette*.

Still, with no official building, each governor was free to place the capital where he wished. When Arthur Dobbs arrived in 1754, he took a quick dislike to New Bern's prices and "miasmic" air. He built his mansion in Brunswick and set up his council and assembly meetings in Wilmington, a few miles away.

Dobbs's death in 1765 brought new hope for prominence in the town of New Bern, and James Davis led the fight with a number of scathing editorials declaring Wilmington a barren wasteland unworthy of leadership position. Of course, the decision would have to be made by the new governor.

William Tryon had arrived, determined to settle this issue once and for all. He had in tow an architect, John Hawks, who would design a governor's mansion and government building that would put most other buildings in the colony to shame. Tryon had not been in the governor's seat long before he was scouring the region for his choice of location.

New Bern's merchants and leaders met the new governor on his way to the town and regaled him and his wife with a banquet and ball. This, and the town's central location, led Tryon to convince the assembly to approve—ultimately—£15,000 to raise Tryon Palace.

Finished in 1770, it was a controversial building. While it definitely settled the capital—for the next fifteen or twenty years, anyway—it was also a massive expenditure for a colony short on funds. By now, the west's population was exploding, and few people in these areas were happy about the permanent establishment of a capital so far away; further, they were already overburdened with taxes, which were often gathered by dishonest collectors who overcharged and didn't always send the money to New Bern. An organized group of men, calling themselves Regulators, rose in protest and ultimately took up arms. In one of his last acts in North Carolina, Governor Tryon met them with his militia near Alamance Creek on May 16, 1771, soundly defeating them and hanging six of their leaders. The movement crushed, Tryon returned home in victory, then in June moved to a new position as governor in New York.

REVOLUTION

North Carolina's last colonial governor, Josiah Martin, was ill fit to handle a colony about to erupt into revolution. It was not long before he was in contention with his assembly and, more often than not, he came out the loser. When the Massachusetts legislature, in 1774, called on all the colonies to send delegates to a Continental Congress in Philadelphia, Martin tried to prevent the election of North Carolina delegates by refusing to summon an assembly. So the assembly met without him—a decidedly illegal act—and chose William Hooper, Richard Caswell and Joseph Hewes as delegates to the first Congress.

Governor Martin's snowball only got larger: in March of 1775 he learned of troops forming against the king; in April his own council deserted him. He called for a general assembly on April 4, and the colonists trumped him by calling another Provincial Congress to meet the day before, denouncing both him and the king in it. Martin set up cannon on the palace's front lawn but townsmen carried them away. The king's authority was gone. Martin sent his family to New York for safety and then, on May 24, fled town to take up residence on a British

Family dynasty. Three generations of Stanlys would leave their indelible mark on New Bern. *Clockwise*: John Wright, privateer and Patriot of the Revolution; his son John, duelist and statesman; and Edward, whose brief service as military governor of North Carolina under Lincoln branded him a traitor by many in the state. *John Wright photo courtesy of Tryon Palace Historic Sites and Gardens; John Stanly photo courtesy of North Carolina Division of Archives; and Edward Stanly photo courtesy of the Library of Congress Prints and Photographs Division, Brady-Handy Photograph Collection.*

ship off Wilmington. From there he spent the next few years trying to convince the British to retake North Carolina for the king.

Her days of freedom were arriving; but New Bern's political glory was on the wane. Richard Caswell, the first governor of the state of North Carolina, resided in the palace, but almost immediately the Provincial Congress moved its meetings inland, to places more defensible from attack.

New Bern was occupied only once, for a couple of days in September 1781, when Tories took over the town. Their chief target was probably John Wright Stanly, who financed a number of privateers against the king. He was in Philadelphia at the time, so they settled for burning his docks and any of his ships they could lay hold of and killing one or two other Patriots they could find.

ANTEBELLUM NEW BERN

Commercially, the town was in its heyday. Numbering about 600 residents in 1770 and nearly 2,500 by 1800, New Bern was the largest town in North Carolina. Its docks were continually busy—there were not only privateers who sailed out (some never to return)

Sunk at the corner of Middle and Pollock Streets as a marker for a survey of the town in 1810, this cannon is one captured by a privateering ship of John Wright Stanly's from a British vessel.

during the Revolution, but also a strong and ongoing trade with America's seaboard towns and the West Indies. As luxury products, spices and fabrics came in, a steady flow of turpentine, lumber and agricultural products went out.

In 1792, the capital was officially moved to Raleigh, a city more centrally located to the shifting populations. The palace, which now served as a school and meeting hall, rapidly deteriorated. (George Washington, who attended a ball there, described it as "a good brick building hastening to ruins.") It took the first step of its phoenix-like existence on February 27, 1798, when it burned to the ground. The lot was subdivided and sold; George Street was extended to run through the spot where the palace had once stood.

Business and culture increased: New Bern in the early 1800s boasted theater performances and traveling wax shows. Steamships arrived in 1817.

New Bern was still a hotbed of politics: many of the state's leaders continued to come from New Bern, among them John Stanly and Richard Dobbs Spaight, who turned to dueling pistols to settle a political argument. Spaight, former governor, and Stanly, a congressman, exchanged four shots each near the Masonic Temple before Stanly's bullet finally found its mark and left the elder ex-governor fatally wounded.

In the early 1800s the fiery-tongued Stanly continued as a powerful force in New Bern. His close friend, the gentler but equally determined

William Gaston, eventually became State Supreme Court judge and the writer of the state song. Indeed, it would not be saying too much to declare this period the era of Stanly and Gaston. Numerous other men of law and politics, ministers, planters, tradesmen and merchants also made their mark in this time—and not to be forgotten was the slave labor upon whose backs much of New Bern's success arose.

1835 was the peak year of New Bern's affluence. The panic of 1837 ushered in a declining economy, and frequent fires plagued the town. As a move to stem its decline, citizens worked to bring a railroad into town. Subscriptions were begun in 1849, and in two

Local artist Willie Taglieri painted this mural on the side of Captain Ratty's Seafood Restaurant, South Front Street, depicting antebellum life in New Bern.

From its founding until the early 1900s, New Bern's docks were a major source of industry and trade. Here, oyster boats await the day's sailing. *Courtesy of North Carolina Division of Archives.*

years $70,000 were raised. In 1853 the Atlantic and North Carolina line was established, tying New Bern to Beaufort and Goldsboro; a New Bernian, John D. Whitford, age twenty-nine, was elected president of the corporation. The townspeople were probably very excited, on a hot June day in 1858, when the railroad finally began to run. In less than four years it would be carrying armed Yankees into town.

THE TOUR

A few of these houses—namely Hay House, the John Wright Stanly House and Tryon Palace (which we will refer to, but which is not technically part of the tour)—are open to the public as part of Tryon Palace Historic Sites and Gardens. If interested, you may purchase a ticket at the visitor center on the corner of George and Pollock Streets. A two-day pass is available and includes several period homes, the New Bern Academy and Tryon Palace itself. Call (252) 514-4000 for details.

To begin your tour, park by Tryon Palace along Eden Street. The first house is located next to the palace parking lot, on your left.

1. Robert Hay House
227 Eden Street
Built 1805

Mr. Hay was already middle-aged when he left Scotland for America around 1800. A good carpenter, he was among the artisans who built the Harvey Mansion, which we shall visit in the Civil War tour.

He bought this house about 1816 and, on October 31, married Nancy Carney, an "old maid" at twenty-five but not nearly so old as her husband, who was then sixty-four. Nancy would bear him five children, the last—a daughter—when he was eighty-one.

A staunch Presbyterian worshipping in a town short on Calvinists, Mr. Hay was one of a select corps who helped to found New Bern's first Presbyterian church in 1817. Though a leader only

Hay descendants enjoy a sunny day at the turn of the twentieth century. *Courtesy of Tryon Palace Historic Sites and Gardens.*

within that church, he was widely loved and respected—when, in his elder years, he was forced to sell his home and its contents for debts (he'd lost a lot of money supporting an errant brother-in-law), the town came together, bought everything back and put it in his wife's name to protect him from losing it again.

Mr. Hay was spoken of extensively in the reminiscences of Stephen W. Miller ("A more devout or better man than Robert Hay has scarcely lived on this earth") and in the Presbyterian church history written by Reverend L.C. Vass in 1886 ("He was early established in sound principles of moral duty and God's providence"), and even in Colonel Whitford's Baptist reminiscences, *The Home Story of a Walking Stick* (fondly noting his fame as "Father Hay").

Mr. Hay's handmade handrails.

His home is a Federal side-hall, wood-framed building. What you see is just as it appeared in 1835, thanks to historic restoration by the palace. Even the plumbing has been removed.

Hay bought the house and lot for $1,000. It was a fixer-upper—no handrails on its precarious, three-story winding stairs, so he built those himself. By the house's original design, the only entrance to the basement kitchen was from outside, so Mr. Hay added an inside stairwell access.

Though a two-story building with side hall and a large room off to the north side on each floor, Mr. Hay's home had a most usable attic, where his sons and apprentices probably slept. Around 1830, after the birth of his daughter Frances, he added a small office (first floor), an additional bedroom (directly above) and a fine, two-story back porch. The addition's exterior wall, facing the porch, was faced with shipboard-style siding, though the rest of the house is in lapboard.

A reproduction period woodstove sits in the basement kitchen.

During the Civil War the home was occupied by Union officers. The Hay family complained that the soldiers had torn down their wooden fence to use as fuel—a famous habit of soldiers of both sides in that war.

Around 1915 a two-story front porch was erected; the back porch was ultimately closed in and additions, including a kitchen, soon wound from the main structure into the backyard. However, the Council of Friends purchased the home in 1994 for Tryon Palace, which in turn devolved the house back to its early incarnation, removing additions, walls, a dormer and the porches. If you wish to visit inside, the home is on display and usually housed with character interpreters who portray the Hays, their servants and family friends of 1835. A ticket is required.

From here, walk north to Pollock Street and turn to your right. In a short distance, George Street T's onto Pollock to your left. Take a moment to look through the palace gates at the Georgian-style Tryon Palace, the recreation of colonial governor William Tryon's government house and home from 1770 to 1771. In its day it was one of the finest buildings in America, and the center of North Carolina government.

When you cross the street you will pass the Tryon Palace visitors' center on your left. The next building is the John Wright Stanly House.

2. John Wright Stanly House
307 George Street
Built circa 1779–83

This house served as the home of a Revolutionary Patriot and an antebellum politician and lawyer—both characters of high note. But it also played a crucial role during the Civil War—crucial enough that we will give it the lone honor of appearing in two separate tours.

Local legend (not evidence) places this house as one designed by John Hawks, designer and builder of Tryon Palace. It is Georgian in style and presently resides at its third address—it was moved twice before, in 1932 and 1966.

John Wright Stanly was a Virginia-born merchant who wound up in New Bern in 1773 as the result of stormy weather and a stormy heart. By that time he had already spent two stints in jail: once on charges of counterfeiting in Williamsburg (he was released unscathed and unconvicted) and once for debt in Philadelphia. He was thrown there as a result of his West Indies trading partner Jonathan Cowpland's accusations, but (largely through his own efforts) was proven misused and innocent.

Doric columns and a fine pediment decorate the Stanly House doorway.

Stanly was sailing for Charleston, South Carolina, when a storm drove his ship into port at Beaufort, North Carolina. From there, local resident and friend John Sitgreaves convinced him to come to New Bern for a visit. At a governor's ball he met a young beauty named Ann Cogdell, fell in love and settled in.

His specialty was the West Indies trade, but King George's navy changed all that. When the Revolution came in, Stanly decided it would be profitable to arm his fleet and engage in privateering. It was a risky venture; like most privateers he lost several ships to British action. In one instance, his ship *Nancy* captured a British sloop, was captured herself while escorting the sloop home and then set free a few days later by a continental ship. He saw part of his fleet burned in New Bern, as well, when the British occupied the town for a day in 1781.

Even so, privateering was a lucrative profession. Stanly built a fortune on it—and with that fortune he helped bankroll General Nathanael Greene's war efforts through a loan that neither he nor his heirs ever saw repaid.

Stanly purchased a large lot on Middle Street from Thomas Ogden (he paid £8,400 proclamation money) in 1779, and there the John Wright Stanly House was built. It features wooden quoins at its corners and, inside, a transverse arch, Greek moldings and pedestal mantels. The central hall is typical Georgian in style.

John Wright Stanly and his wife, Anne, both died of yellow fever during an epidemic in 1789 and were buried in the Christ Church yard. For a few years while their eldest son, John, waited to come of age, the house stood empty. It was during this time that, according to tradition, George Washington stayed at the house during his 1791 tour. He referred in his journal to having "exceeding good" accommodations here. However, research papers at Tryon Palace, which now owns the building, cast possible doubt as to whether this was, indeed, that "exceeding good" house.

John Stanly, the lawyer, took the house when he came of age. He was one of the two most famous lawyers in town (the other was his close friend, William Gaston). Stanly was known for his deeply sarcastic and withering regard of all opponents, and spent many years serving his town in both Congress and the North Carolina assembly.

Stanly was most famous, however, for his duel with Richard Dobbs Spaight, the elder former governor of North Carolina. Spaight was no cooler of temperament than Stanly and, after feeling his character had been expunged, launched into a war of letters with Stanly. These gravitated to handbills and newspaper reprints and finally to a duel held near the Masonic Hall and theater in town. They fired four rounds before one finally fell. In one exchange, Stanly's coat collar was shot; but in the end it was Spaight who was mortally

The recreated Stanly study.

wounded. Stanly fled the state briefly but convinced the governor to pardon his act.

One other character of note lived at the house during the antebellum years, if only for a few days. Stanly's daughter, Elizabeth, had enraged her father by marrying a War of 1812 veteran named Walker Keith Armistead. It is by no means certain why Stanly took a disliking to the man—he had distinguished himself in that war and would end his life as second in command of the U.S. Army in 1845.

Elizabeth was visiting home with her unwelcome husband on February 18, 1817, when she went into labor and delivered a son whose name was Lewis Addison Armistead. Forty-six years later Lewis would find himself dressed in gray, leading hordes of ill-fated men up Cemetery Hill at Gettysburg: he was leading Picket's Charge, his hat on the end of his waving sword. Though the charge would prove disastrous, a few of his men managed to cross the Union lines before retreating or being captured or killed. Armistead was one who made it, but he was mortally wounded. To this epic disaster and accomplishment goes the high watermark of the Civil War.

John Stanly died—the long effects of a stroke—in 1833; the following year his heirs sold the house to other families. Among its future owners were descendants of Richard Dobbs Spaight.

The John Wright Stanly House is currently restored to its eighteenth-century splendor and is beautifully furnished with antiques and original paintings of John and Anne Stanly, as well as some of their children. It is open for visiting as part of the Tryon Palace Historic Sites and Gardens tour.

Our next house is a remarkably easy walk: it's next door.

3. John Daves House
313 George Street
Built circa 1770

It has spread all over the place now, with additions working their way into the backyard, then turning a sharp left. Viewed from the air, this house in its present shape forms a primitive, reverse-image "C." John Daves pretty much built it himself: a little Georgian cottage within view of the fabulous and then brand-new Tryon Palace, a place he would come to rue.

John was a hero in the Revolution. A soldier in the Continental line, he was named quartermaster of the Second Regiment. He fought with

Gables on the John Daves house.

Washington's forces at Brandywine and Germantown, froze at Valley Forge and was wounded at Stony Point in 1779.

Following the war John continued as a major of North Carolina state troops. In 1790 he became the first collector of customs at the port of New Bern. The state also appointed him, in 1778, caretaker of the vacated and deteriorating palace—perhaps some bright legislator thought it would be a lark for him, being a couple of stone's throws from his front door. Considering the palace's problems of leakage and its unorthodox, post-colonial use as everything from a dance school to a kind of market, he was probably tempted to throw those stones.

The original cottage is side-hall, with the stairwell on the south side; it has one of the most steeply pitched roofs in town, and a fine, unique, original chimney centrally located to better heat the home.

Sadness reached John's home: his first wife, Sally Bryan, died shortly after the birth of their daughter, Mary, in 1776 (making for a bittersweet celebration of independence, indeed). He would wed again, this time to Mary Haynes Long Davis, who would outlive Major Daves by five years.

Five children were raised within these walls; all would marry well, and one son (Thomas Haynes Daves) would become a Craven County sheriff.

Continue following George Street—across Broad Street (Tabernacle Baptist is on your right). At the next intersection (New Street), turn right. Walk to the corner of New and Metcalf Streets. On your right, across the road, is our next home.

4. Hawks House
517 New Street
Built circa 1760–69. Moved 1975.

Here is a unique old house (one of only two like it in town), dwelled in at one time by the son of the most famous architect in colonial North Carolina—and the father of the historian-pastor who would buy the gates of Cedar Grove Cemetery and one day scandalize New York.

If you carve off two-fifths of the Hawks House in your mind's eye and then lift the whole thing up and drop it over on Hancock Street, you will get a good idea of how it looked when it was new. The original lot was bought by the well-to-do merchant and Patriot John Green and may have had the beginnings of the house already standing. If so, Green added extensively, coming up with this Georgian gambrel-roofed domicile.

In his hands, it was a social hot spot. Philadelphia journal writer William Attmore, in 1787, noted a visit to New Bern in which Mr. Green was one of his hosts. On November 23, after watching a horse named Sweeper win a race, he "Went to Dine with John Green, by invitation; there was Miss Cogdell, Misses Wright Stanly, Mr. Dolley, & Mr. _____ Green (John's brother)—Towards evening took a walk with John Green to see the palace." As to the Cogdells and "Misses Wright Stanly," they were the daughters of the rich and powerful Richard Cogdell—you would not find them at just *any* gathering. Later, William would breakfast with Green, and later yet turn down an invitation from him to attend church.

In 1807, some time after Mr. Green passed away, Francis Hawks—customs collector for New Bern and the son of the architect who'd built Tryon Palace—purchased the house. He had five children—his son, Francis Lister Hawks, among them—and it is likely that having so many people bumping about the place convinced him, sometime between 1810 and 1820, that it was time to add on, resulting in the house you see today.

Francis was apparently a believer in "spare the rod, spoil the child." Colonel Whitford would write that Francis's son "would often playfully tell of his stern father 'tuning up' his boys Monday morning and when innocence was offered to prevent it would be told, 'Oh, you will deserve it anyway before the week is half gone.'"

That son, Francis Lister, grew up to pursue a career in law where he "at once stood among the leaders of his profession," Stephen W. Miller remembered. "His voice was the richest imaginable, his language copious and beautiful, and his manner very impressive." In 1821 he became a state legislator, representing New Bern, married a Northerner in 1823 and soon moved on to Hillsboro. In 1827 he had an epiphany, turned to ministry and wound up an Episcopal rector in New York. Through the years he focused his attention on education and made frequent visits back to New Bern, where he often spoke and was always received with honors. He became an important historian of the denomination as well, and wrote histories on North Carolina.

Midway through Francis Lister's career, scandals cropped up: a minstrel performer named George Washington Dixon accused him of adultery. Hawks denied it and charged Dixon with libel (Dixon pled guilty); later, his boys' school in Long Island faced financial problems and Hawks was accused of mismanaging the funds. He struggled with personal finances as well. He died shortly after the Civil War, in 1866, and is buried in Greenwich, Connecticut.

This house is Georgian, although there are Federal touches (inside and out), courtesy of Mr. Hawks. It was moved to its present location in 1975.

Continue down to the end of the block. On your right, across from the New Bern Academy, is our next stop.

5. Stanly-Bishop House
501 New Street
Built circa 1810

Antebellum New Bern was unique in its opportunities for African Americans. Though steeped in slavery, this "Athens of the South" boasted the highest percentage of free blacks in any North Carolina town. In 1820, for instance, of 3,663 counted residents, 2,188 were black (almost 62 percent of the population). Of those, 268 were freedmen (12 percent of the black population). And of those 268 freedmen, several were surprisingly well-to-do. A few owned slaves themselves.

Among these freedmen, Stephen Miller mentions five as examples, including Dunum Mumford, a "copper-colored" bricklayer; Sylvester Pimborton, a butcher, "uniformly patient and accommodating"; John Carruthers Stanly, a barber and master of several plantations; and John Stewart Stanly, his son.

Colonel Whitford, in his reminiscences, also mentioned an Asa Spelman who not only fought in the Revolutionary War, but was also an acquaintance of George Washington.

Of the freedmen Miller mentions, at least three (both of the Stanlys and Mumford) owned slaves. At one time, J.C. Stanly was one of the largest slaveholders in the state. Curiously, he was born into slavery in 1772, the son of an Ebo slave woman and—reputedly—the privateer-merchant John Wright Stanly. He gained his freedom—depending on the source used—in 1798 or 1808 and began his new life as a barber, known to one and all as "Barber Jack."

This stop on the tour was actually Barber Jack's house. Owning sixty or more slaves and three plantations, he was an anomaly of black life in the South: a successful and respected leader ("a man of dignified presence, [who] lived in fashionable style, his sons and daughters were well educated, and always making a good appearance

From his front step, John C. Stanly could see the church he had helped found.

as bright mulattoes," Stephen Miller would recall). Not everyone would so appreciate him. The Confederate colonel John D. Whitford, in his writings, recalled, "He was in the day's of his prosperity popular with the negroes with whom he would no more associate than would the most respectable white man. He was a hard task master. Finally however, being overwhelmed with reverses and debt dying insolvent after scattering a few of his negroes among his children." (He did die poor; but at least part of that was the fault of loans he'd made to his half-brother, John Stanly the lawyer, that had gone bad).

Stanly purchased the freedom of several family members (including his wife) and freed a few others—but by no means all—of his slaves for meritorious service.

Over time, the number of blacks holding slaves would decrease: only eight black North Carolinians held them in 1860, and only one in New Bern—Stanly's daughter Catherine, who controlled the lives of seven African Americans when the war broke out.

Stanly was a cofounder of the First Presbyterian Church. Kitty, his wife, is memorialized on a stone plaque there. It was a convenient walk to church from his home; in fact, he could look to his right and see it the next block over, whenever he stepped out of his house.

He bought this house in 1815 and lived there until 1831 when finances and other considerations forced him to sell to one Matthew Outten. In 1875 the house was sold to the carpenter George Bishop, the contractor who oversaw the rebuilding of Christ Church, and it is from him that this house takes the second part of its name.

In its original condition it was Federal, four bays wide, with a two-story porch crossing the back of the building. It was enlarged sometime after 1830 (probably by Outten) and then again after 1913 and 1931.

Walk two more blocks down New and you will come upon a long, two-story, yellow house. This is at the intersection of New and Craven Streets, and it is best viewed from Craven Street.

6. Gaston House
421 Craven Street
Built circa 1769

James Coor built this house about the same time that John Hawks built the governor's mansion a few blocks away. Coor was the same architect who built the Coor-Bishop mansion on East Front Street (which we examine in another tour). He built this as his own home and asked that he and his wife be buried in the garden.

James Coor was a statesman and Patriot. A member of colonial Governor Tryon's general assembly, he was also among those, in August of 1774, who elected North Carolina's first delegates to the Continental Congress. According to Colonel Whitford—whose colonial facts are sometimes suspect—James Coor was an immigrant from England who arrived in New Bern at the behest of Thomas

Entryway to the Gaston House today.

Weber, who was looking for a good architect (perhaps John Hawks was too busy putting up the governor's "palace" at the time).

Coor willed this house to his niece, a lady with the tongue-tangling name of Sarah Groenendkye. Her heirs sold it to its most famous residents, the statesman and lawyer William Gaston, on April 17, 1818.

Gaston—who was a state assemblyman, founder of the first official Catholic congregation in North Carolina and writer of the state song (to be adopted in 1926)—was in particular need of a town house, for he had just married his third wife and had a growing brood of children to shelter.

Though a slave owner himself, Gaston is recognized in part for the strong stands he took in favor of the black race. When, in 1835, the

The Gaston House when it served as a Union hospital in the Civil War.
Courtesy of Massachusetts MOLLUS Photograph Collection, U.S. Military History Institute, Carlisle Barracks, Pennsylvania.

state constitution was rewritten to disenfranchise free blacks, Gaston (who served on the constitutional committee) was among the loudest in opposition. Though he lost that battle, he was able to remove from the constitution a former law requiring acceptance of Protestant doctrine to hold office in the state.

The Gaston house is curiously abutted with the sidewalks on Craven and Johnson Streets. Its relatively plain exterior is brightened up by a fine pair of Diocletian attic windows and, according to Gaston's biographer J. Herman Schauinger, a "double veranda [that] had a delicate railing, cunningly wrought, considered by many to be superior to that of the famous Stanly home."

The long addition, which nearly doubles the house's size, was added on about 1850, some years after Gaston's death. Its size probably had much to do with the fact that it became the Foster General Hospital during the Civil War.

From Gaston House walk westward (away from downtown) and keep an eye out on your right for 514 Craven Street. It is a smaller house, tucked in amidst its larger neighbors.

7. James Bright House
514 Craven Street
Built circa 1790

This quaint little gambrel-roofed Georgian house is most notable for its habit of lifting up its foundations and moving around town. It has happened four times to date—not even the John Wright Stanly House, with three moves, can match it.

The James Bright House

ca. 1790

Relocated & Restored 1973

Private Residence

New Bern settled 1710

Historical Point of Interest

It started life at the corner of Broad and Bern Streets as a quiet little cottage built for James Bright. His was a fairly large family—by 1790 he and his wife had two sons, five daughters and eight slaves. He may be the same James Bright who was a captain in the Dobbs Militia from 1771 to 1774 and who probably served in some capacity in the Revolutionary War.

James and his family owned the house through 1796, though they moved to Lenoir County by 1786. While living there they sold the home to the Patriot John Daves for £60. Over the next several years the house changed ownership several times.

By 1908, the house had shifted locations for the first time, over to a smaller lot on Broad Street. In 1967 the New Bern Historical Society took over the house, moving it to society property behind the Attmore-Oliver House (located on Broad Street). Finally, in 1973, the house was moved a final time to its present Craven Street location.

The Bright House underwent major changes after its 1973 move, including rear and side additions, although the main structure still gives a reasonably accurate picture of its original appearance.

Follow Craven Street to King Street and turn right. At the end of the block turn right onto East Front Street. When you reach the Rains brothers' historic marker, you will see the next house a door or two farther down, on the east side of the street.

8. Salter's Store
604 East Front Street
Built circa 1800–40

With its bright blue double doors and old-world charm, this house—once a store—may have you looking about for Amish residents tinkering in the yard.

It likely started life as a one-story building, the store of Elijah Clark, who along with Mary Mitchell and John Brinson founded the town's first Baptist church in his home. As Peter B. Sandebeck points out, the lot was deeded to him in 1818. Stephen F. Miller, in his recollections, talks of Elijah and his son, William, running a store "up the Neuse… They were good merchants, and had a large country trade."

A second story and a business-like false façade were added about mid-century and, later, a two-story side porch was attached.

William Salter and George Slover purchased the store in 1872 and Salter ran it for many years, from whence it picked up its name.

In a way, it seems an odd place for a store in the early to mid-1800s. Most of the business in New Bern was well down the road, at the confluence of East and South Streets. There, the oyster boats shelled out their wares and the steamers and small sailboats arrived with passengers and goods from New York and Jamaica. And this, the 600 block of East Front Street, though near water, was practically on the far edge of town. Perhaps that "large country trade" went to Elijah's place because the farmers preferred to avoid the hustle and bustle.

The gable-front store is fairly typical of nineteenth-century businesses in New Bern. Its double door and display windows reveal the home for what it used to be.

Continue down East Front Street. The next house is on the left.

9. Eli Smallwood House
521 East Front Street
Built circa 1810–12

The Eli Smallwood House and (behind it) the Jones Jarvis House. The two houses are nearly identical.

While President Madison (very unpopular in New Bern, by the way) worked his way toward declaring war with England, Asa King was raising this house, "the epitome," Peter Sandbeck declares, "of the stylish New Bern Federal side-hall plan house." It is, in fact, practically a twin of its next-door neighbor, the Jones-Jarvis House (1810–11), at 528 East Front Street. As Sandbeck notes, it was a popular form of design in this town during those years; at least three other homes mimicked it.

This lot had been a tanyard run by Colonel Joseph Leech before Eli Smallwood purchased it in 1807. He was a merchant in town and, more notably, a planter outside of it. Stephen Miller recalled, "Eli Smallwood was successful in accumulating property. His marriage with

A 1934 Bayard Wootten photograph of the Eli Smallwood stairwell. *Courtesy of Library of Congress.*

Mrs. Blackwell, a Northern lady, took place just before my removal from Newbern, and his character for shrewd financial management was then well-established, although he was not, in 1824, probably over thirty years of age." He further described Eli, at least in those younger days, as "a fine looking gentleman."

It was not unusual for planters to take up residences in town. The martyred Patriot Alexander Gaston had such a residence and died because he was there instead of at his plantation house when the Tories arrived in town. Miller lists nine "planters residing in town," including community leaders George Pollock ("among the wealthiest men of the State"), John P. Daves ("who held the highest rank in society") and Asa Jones ("a goodly specimen of the wise planter and the courteous city gentleman").

Based on early maps, Mr. Smallwood kept warehouses and wharves out back—they do not survive today.

The entranceway is a Palladian-form portico; the interiors with their fine molded fireplace mantels are intricately wrought. At one time the parlor was Eli's counting room, but looking at this house one gets no impression of a Scrooge-like figure hunched over his ledger books and grumbling about the cost of poorhouses. The whole home suggests an aura of quiet tranquility—the very image of New Bern in its antebellum years.

Continue down East Front Street about three houses on the left to our last home.

10. Gull Harbor
514 East Front Street
Built circa 1815–18

Here is where, a plaque tells us, Elizabeth Shine, mother of the Yankee Civil War hero Admiral David Farragut, was born in 1765. Was she? If so, it was obviously not in this building, as its Federal style alone assures us it was built well after that date.

The property was in the hands of one William Blackledge, an up-and-coming lawyer and future congressman, in 1815 when it was sold to Increase Bradley. If there was a house then, it must have been torn down to make way for this one.

As for Elizabeth Shine, she married the forty-year-old Jorge Farragut—a Spaniard who had come to America to fight the Revolution—and moved to Tennessee (at that time part of North Carolina), where she gave birth to her famous son.

One of the home's fine fireplaces. The portrait is of Penelope Barker, an ancestor of the current owners and a participant in the Edenton Tea Party of 1774.

The biggest problem with claims of Elizabeth having been born in New Bern arises from Jorge's family Bible, which states (in Spanish) that "Elizabeth Shine was born in the State of North Carolina, Dobs CO, near Kinston, over the Neuse River, June 7, 1765." By the 1790 census, Dobbs County was *part* of the New Bern district, but it wasn't New Bern itself. Unless there is an error in that transcription, she was *almost* born in New Bern—but not quite.

By 1808 the family resided in New Orleans, which was not a particularly good thing for Elizabeth: she died of yellow fever there and David was adopted by a man named David Porter. This hardship would prove his blessing, for Porter took the boy to sea. In the War of 1812 Porter captained the USS *Essex*; he captured a British vessel and placed twelve-year-old David in command of the captured ship, which he sailed safely to port.

If, however, Farragut's mother *was* born in New Bern, it adds an interesting touch of irony, for the torpedoes that Farragut damned in his 1864 assault on Mobile Bay were invented by New Bernian Gabriel Rains, just up the street.

As to the house before us: it is Federal style, two and a half stories, with a basement that includes a cooking kitchen. It is side-hall and, originally, its entranceway opened directly onto East Front Street (it now faces south). It includes a pair of richly decorated fireplaces.

The name of Gull Harbor is new—relatively speaking, for that little "harbor" (which runs along Council Bluff park) did not come into being until about 1920, when it was dug to serve as a coast guard dock.

The current owners have a fine portrait of their ancestor, Penelope Barker. Penelope, the wife of colony treasurer Thomas Barker, made a hero of herself in America (and a pariah in England) by organizing the Edenton Tea Party of October 25, 1774, against the king's Tea Act of 1773, convincing her fellow female Edentonians to boycott British tea. It was an event angrily lampooned in the British press. The more theatrical and better-known Boston Tea Party took place ten months earlier, in October 1773.

It is time to return to the palace—and here is your longest walk. Continue down East Front Street, walking past the Sudan Shrine Temple and around the circle. At the next block you will come to Pollock Street; turn right. Take this for five blocks (you will pass the palace entrance on your left) and turn left at Eden Street. Here you will return to your car.

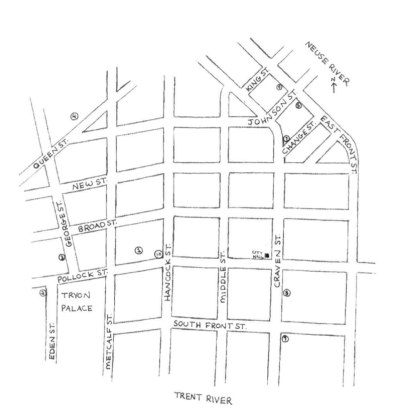

The Civil War

New Bern would be a boon to both sides of the "War of Northern Aggression." To the South, she would give talent and blood: a handful of officers, numerous soldiers, some spies and two men (raised here, though no longer residents) who would do much for the defense of the Confederacy through the production of gunpowder and the invention of arms. Even the North would gain a leader in the form of Ed Stanly, grandson of the Revolutionary privateer John Wright Stanly. A Unionist, he would return from California to serve as military governor here.

The appearance of a railroad—at last—seemed to promise a new day for the city. A new branch of the State Bank had just opened in town with Edward R. Stanly (no relation to the governor) as president. As of September 1859 the citizens were taking nighttime strolls down gaslit streets and reading into the morning hours by the glow of gas lanterns in their homes.

On May 17, 1861, New Bern's John D. Whitford, the young president of the Atlantic and North Carolina Railroad, was on hand in Raleigh to cast his ballot for secession. The vote carried. Three days later, the eastern half of Virginia followed suit (her western counties quickly formed their own, pro-Union government and seceded from the state).

Theater remained an integral part of town at the start of the war: that comic hit

This map of New Bern was drawn by a member of the Forty-fourth Massachusetts Regiment in 1863. Along with some buildings, it also shows the location of several forts (Fort Totten, at left, is today a playground and park). *Courtesy of New Bern Historical Society.*

Our American Cousin was performed by the Bailey Troupe a good four years before the April 1865 performance that would sear an otherwise mediocre play into American historical lore.

In business, turpentine, not cotton, was king. Oyster harvesting, lumber and plantations provided business for incoming and outgoing ships. The shores were almost clogged with docks, sails and the smoke of chugging steamboats. Women strolled and shopped; fishmongers shouted their wares; cats, dogs and gulls hunted for scraps and unwatched produce.

Aside from loved ones on the battlefield, New Bern remained relatively unscathed during the opening months of the war—although a mutton-chopped fellow named Ambrose Burnside was causing some concern as he slowly guided his army down the Carolina coast, making the Outer Banks a Union bastion as he moved along. Already, Virginia had begun siphoning off manpower wherever it could. Most North Carolina regiments were tramping about the fields and forests of Manassas and Seven Pines. Only a handful—mostly untried—was left to defend their home state.

In March 1862 it came to a head as General Burnside brought his gunboats up the Neuse River, ready to tackle his primary target. On March 13 he began landing three brigades—twelve thousand men—a few miles below the town.

The Confederates' situation was already dire. Ill equipped and low on arms (many of their exploding cannonballs, for lack of powder, had been stuffed with sand), 4,500 inexperienced men under the command of their

GENERAL BURNSIDE'S PRIVATE CARRIAGE.

A humorous etching by Vincent Colyer, superintendent of the poor, suggests the "elaborate" transportation General Burnside often used while he was still in charge of Union-occupied New Bern. *Etching from* Report of the Services Rendered to the Freed People, *Vincent Colyer, 1864.*

equally inexperienced and untrained politician-general, Lawrence O. Branch, awaited the onslaught.

Next day the armies clashed, with well-equipped Union men charging with their deadly Springfield and Enfield muskets into a mass of defenders armed mainly with flintlocks and civilian guns. Under the circumstances, the Rebs did well: for four hours they slugged it out. Colonel Zebulon Vance, with his Twenty-seventh North Carolina and a portion of the Thirty-third, heroically held off vastly superior forces, buying time for their fellow soldiers and the residents of New Bern to flee the doomed town.

In the end, the Athens of the South fell to the Spartans of the North. Residents and soldiers leaped onto railroad cars that hurried them out of town; two cars got uncoupled, stranding civilians who took refuge in the Moses Griffin School. Later, Burnside allowed them to flee.

A widows' walk is not enough. To gain elevation for the signal corps, awkward-looking platforms were sometimes built onto existing widows' walks, as on the Jones-Jarvis House at 528 East Front Street. *Courtesy of Massachusetts MOLLUS Photograph Collection, U.S. Military History Institute, Carlisle Barracks, Pennsylvania.*

From this point forward New Bern became the Union base of operations for North Carolina. Soon the number of Union troops in New Bern (twenty thousand) would outnumber the Confederate forces defending the entire state.

Under a series of commanders, various expeditions set out from New Bern to Goldsboro, Kinston, Washington and other towns. Happily for the South, most (at least early in the war) were of questionable success.

Mixing with the Union forces were persons of every color and profession: residents (mostly poor) who remained behind, sutlers, missionaries, tradesmen and blacks—thousands of "contraband" slaves who fled to the Union bastion to embrace their freedom. Even before the war, New Bern had the highest percentage of freedmen in any North Carolina town (689 of 2,409 blacks in the county were free—about 29 percent). Here they settled within Union lines, most working to build a new life. Forts and trestles rose from their paid labor. Soon, James City, a community for blacks, was started, and in April of 1863 the "African Brigade" was authorized by Secretary of War Edwin Stanton. Three North Carolina regiments and the Fifty-first Massachusetts formed the unit. These soldiers not only performed provost duty, but also proved themselves in excursions and the defense of the town.

Houses, churches and halls were converted to every possible military use as headquarters, barracks, hospitals and warehouses. Observation towers were built on top of widows' walks and boards were laid across pews as makeshift hospital beds. It is hard to find a period house that didn't serve some such function at the time.

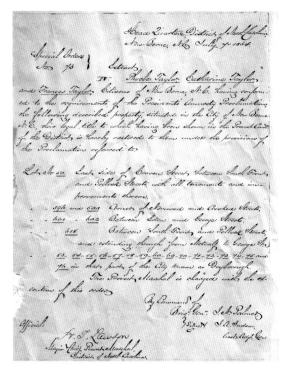

To regain control of their homes, New Bernians ultimately had to sign an oath of loyalty to the Union. The Taylor sisters regained control of the Isaac Taylor House in this way in 1864. *Courtesy of Paul Switzer.*

As with any standing army of the day, disease was a major concern, killing more men than any bullets or cannonballs. A major yellow fever epidemic swept the town in the fall of 1864, indiscriminately killing Southerners and Yankees alike. One regiment, the Fifteenth Connecticut, lost over 140 men to "Yellow Jack."

Twice Confederates attempted to retake the town, but their efforts failed. After the war, New Bern remained in occupied hands for several months. Many of the soldiers who served here took a liking to the place and returned to live. Things would never be the same.

CIVIL WAR TOUR

How do you narrow down dozens of qualifying houses to a manageable ten? It's no easy task. The tales of many that didn't make it here are so intriguing it hurts to leave them out. A couple—homes that were primary headquarters—had to be included. This is why the John Wright Stanly House shows up again. The Slover House, headquarters for General Foster (and also the probable setting of a Mark Twain story), was also an obvious choice. The Rains brothers' childhood home is included because of the contribution those boys made to the Southern cause.

Other homes appear because of the colorful people involved, or the interesting anecdotes available. One makes the cut because of its interesting architecture, not studied elsewhere.

This 1864 lithograph shows New Bern's busy rivers during occupation times. *Courtesy of North Carolina Division of Archives.*

You may also browse over First Baptist, St. Peter's AME Zion, Christ Church and First Presbyterian in the "Houses of Worship" section and read about their Civil War ties. We have also discussed the Gaston House's wartime function in the "Colonial–Antebellum" tour.

Another prominent building we do not include is St. John's Masonic Lodge, which served as a hospital and wartime theater. The New Bern Academy (part of the Tryon Palace complex) houses a fine Civil War museum. If you are interested, you may call offices at either place for details on their history.

To begin your tour, park at the historical society (located at 510 Pollock Street). Although the address of our first house is technically on Broad Street, the easiest access to it is from this parking lot, walking into the backyard. You can easily stroll around the front, and tours of the home are available (call the society office at (252) 633-1614 for information).

1. Attmore-Oliver House
513 Broad Street
Built circa 1790–1800

This home is brought to you by our love for our past. Built about 1790 by Revolutionary War veteran Samuel Chapman, it would go on to have its history in the Civil War as well.

Chapman was a friend—or at least acquaintance—of George Washington. When the president made his Southern tour in 1791, Chapman represented St. John's Masonic Lodge before him. He was a successful businessman and merchant, owning a plantation outside town and, at his death, twenty-one slaves. He was also a founding member of one of the city's earliest insurance businesses, the Newbern Marine Insurance Company.

Looking upon the house, you will see little of Chapman's original humble structure, a one-and-a-half-story dwelling in which he lived until his death. His daughter, Caroline Chapman, inherited it in 1806.

Front and back views of the Attmore-Oliver House show a difference in architectural styles.

Isaac Taylor, a maritime merchant, purchased the house in 1834. He did not need it for himself, having a fine brick home on Craven Street (we visit it later in this tour). However, he had in mind a wedding gift for his daughter, Mary, who had just wed George Sitgreaves Attmore, a businessman with Philadelphia roots. He bought the house and began extensive renovations, turning it into the three-story structure currently on display. The happy couple moved in, but Taylor kept the title.

It is a curious house. The Broad Street side—its front—is Greek Revival with a Tuscan portico, Doric columns and floor-length windows. The back—accessed by a driveway off Pollock Street—is quite another story: Federal style with a broad two-floor porch and flush-style siding.

The Attmores received the house on Taylor's death in 1846, and then passed it on to their daughter, Hannah Taylor Attmore Oliver, in 1860.

The south foyer leads to the second floor.

A number of the Attmore-Olivers signed up to fight in the Civil War. Hannah's husband, William, served as a Confederate quartermaster. Her three brothers also joined, meeting various fates: Sitgreaves Attmore, captured in the Battle of Fort Fisher south of Wilmington in 1865, died of dysentery while a prisoner of war; Isaac Attmore died at Spotsylvania Court House in 1864 while fighting with the Beaufort Rifles; and George, just thirteen when the war began, was an artillerist whose company witnessed the war's end at Appomattox Court House (he would live out his life in New Bern).

The house remained in Oliver hands until 1951, when the last of the Olivers to live there, Miss Mary Oliver, willed it to five nephews who lived in Fayetteville. These nephews in turn sold the house to the historic society in 1953 for $30,000 and since then this grounds—including the Roberts House at 512 Pollock Street—has become headquarters of the society. Restorations have been an ongoing project and the house now features period furnishings, portraits of some of the original dwellers, a fine antique doll collection and one room dedicated exclusively to artifacts of the Civil War. Among the artifacts is a rare, seven-star Confederate flag. Abandoned by retreating Rebels, the banner had been taken as a souvenir by Thomas Merrill, a Connecticut soldier. It was donated to the society by one of his descendants in 1967. The seven stars represented the original seven states that had seceded from the union.

Going back to Pollock Street, turn right and walk past the Tryon Palace entrance (on your left). You will notice the Dixon House to the left of the entrance; this home served as a hospital during the Civil War. Continue to the end of this block (walking on the south side of the street), and you will come to Eden Street. Across the street is our second stop.

2. Jones House
231 Eden Street
Built circa 1809

A 1903 calendar leaf showing Jones House, looking very much as it does today, and its most famous prisoner, the Southern spy Emiline Pigott. *Courtesy of North Carolina Division of Archives.*

A fine old two-porch dwelling, enlarged around 1820, this home was built for a well-to-do, church-minded turpentine distiller who was one of the original founders of the Presbyterian church. He would live out his years here until 1840, and his descendants after him until 1920. His name was John Jones.

But the house's best-known resident stayed there only a short time— and then against her will.

Still, let's start our story with John. His descendants were Quakers who had settled the area about 1710, just in time to be surprised at a tar-kiln by marauding Indians in the Tuscarora war of 1711. One was decapitated, and the Indians whacked his head around for a while with the kiln's stirring stick.

Jones apparently picked up on that ancestor's career, while nicely avoiding his fate. He was also an active Mason and a stockholder of the New Bern Library Company. Stephen Miller, in his reminiscences of New Bern life in the 1820s, spoke of his distillery as if Mr. Jones were making high-priced aftershave: "When the wind passed over them, the atmosphere in the vicinity was pleasant and refreshing from the odors exhaled as the stills were emptied of their boiling contents, and the pure rosin remained in solution."

Jones's neighbor to the south was Robert Hay, carriage maker and fellow founder of the church. Though older, Hay would be a pallbearer at Jones's funeral and outlive him by twelve years.

When the town fell to General Burnside and his troops, the Yankees decided that Mr. Jones's house would make a fine "secesh" prison. It must have been well known, for a number of photographs and sketches exist of it from this period.

The Yankees rarely had a problem finding prisoners to keep. Sympathizers needed arresting and spies needed to be tracked down. Though many Southerners had fled the city upon its capture, plenty still remained. Some of these were virulent enough against their hosts that they were willing to collect information and pass it beyond Union lines—often with good effect.

Women, especially, were recruited. They carried letters back and forth, both of a military and of a more innocent nature; they also carried clothing, medicine and other supplies across Union lines or to prisoners, filling their ample hoop skirts with the contraband items.

One such woman was Mrs. Alexander Taylor, who gained permission from her father's friend, Governor Edward Stanly, to visit the prisoners about town. She took to carrying illicit mail in her false pockets. A Federal officer joined her along the street one day and said, "Mrs. Taylor, it is very strange, but we cannot find out how or where this Rebel mail comes in or who receives it." She stood shocked, not knowing whether he was simply making conversation or accusing her.

Deciding to "bull" her way through, she brightly confessed, "Why I receive it and at this moment my pockets are full of letters. Would you like to see them?"

He laughed, she laughed and he passed on. She passed the letters on.

One of the prisoners she often visited was another woman—the one most associated with Jones House. That was Emiline Pigott, a Carteret County resident who'd lost her beau to the battlefield. Emiline had taken to carrying letters and dispatches, many of them regarding military information about New Bern.

She was finally arrested and searched (she ate an important letter in the process) and was found to be carrying a veritable stockpile of supplies on her person, including boots. Imprisoned in Jones House, she could have awaited her fate as a spy—which could easily have been hanging. Instead, she contacted various influential men she knew in New Bern. They were compromised, she reminded them—traitors who'd given her information. If she went to trial, there might be more than just *her* pretty neck in a hemp collar. Taking the hint, they applied appropriate pressure, and Emiline was finally freed.

Mr. Jones's house is Georgian in style, but with Federal interior woodwork. You can visit part of it today, for the front room serves as a spacious gift shop for Tryon Palace Historic Sites and Gardens.

Cross Pollock Street and walk past the palace visitors' center, turning left at the corner (George Street). The next house on your left is our third stop.

3. John Wright Stanly House
307 George Street
Built circa 1779–83

GENERAL BURNSIDE'S HEADQUARTERS, NEWBERN, N. C.

This Vincent Colyer etching shows the Stanly House at its New and Middle Street location, when it served as General Burnside's headquarters in 1862. Later in the war it would become a convent for nuns. *Etching from* Report of the Services Rendered to the Freed People, *Vincent Colyer, 1864.*

We have spoken of this house's creation and architectural style in the "Colonial–Antebellum" tour, so you may want to turn there to learn its early history. Here, we will look at its place in the Civil War.

Located at that time on Middle Street (where the Federal Building now stands), it was one of the finest mansions in town, so it only made sense that the military would quickly snatch it up as a headquarters.

On March 14, 1862, the city fell and the Yankees poured into New Bern. When General John G. Foster took over the district from General Ambrose Burnside (who'd been shipped north to the Army of the Potomac), he quickly set up headquarters in the mansion—only to give it up in October to the Sisters of Mercy, who'd moved into town from Beaufort.

These sisters—almost buried alive in their hot, cascading garments and habits—had sailed south from New York City in July of 1862 to help tend wounded and ailing soldiers. Efficient, loving and determined, they turned the mansion into a convent. "We were agreeably surprised" by the accommodations, Sister Augustine, who headed the order, wrote. According to architectural historian Peter

Sandbeck, the home has pattern-book interiors that are "the most sophisticated in New Bern" and could not help but please. The sisters converted the "magnificent drawing room" into a chapel and worshipped in an environment where "gorgeous roses cluster around and climb into the windows and mocking-birds fluttering through the branches serenade the Sisters at their prayers, while two majestic trees, 'The Pride of India'—stand sentinels of honor before the entrance." Apparently the home had quite a garden in those days.

Following the war, the house continued to go through new owners until James A. Bryan purchased it in 1884. He made several additions to the place; then, in 1932, his heirs sold it to the government, which built the Federal Building on its site, moving the house to a new location on the same grounds. There, it became the city's library.

Photographer Matthew Brady's portrait of General Ambrose Burnside. *Courtesy of Library of Congress, Prints and Photographs Division.*

By this time the house had gone through numerous social transitions: from a home to a military headquarters, to convent, to a home again and finally a library.

In 1966, the Stanly House took on its last and, possibly, finest persona: the Library Association, having decided to raise a new building, donated the home to Tryon Palace Historic Sites and Gardens, on the promise that it would be restored and displayed as a museum piece. The house was moved to its present location and opened to the public in all its eighteenth-century glory. It is well worth a visit today.

Continue along George Street, crossing Broad Street. Continue two more blocks and you will come upon the police station on your left—and Cedar Grove Cemetery on your right. Enter the cemetery through its central stone gates along Queen Street.

4. Cedar Grove Cemetery
Queen Street
Established 1799

This picturesque cemetery is the storing house of many of New Bern's greatest names. Walking down the oyster-shell drive you will pass tombstones both classic and modern, statuesque and Doric, simple in comment and eloquent of speech.

A Civil War soldier's rendition of the Weeping Gates. *Courtesy of Tryon Palace Historic Sites and Gardens.*

Here rest lawyers, inventors, artists and statesmen—powerful magnates and common men, women and children. It could easily fall under any walking tour, but we have reserved it for the Civil War tour because of its honored Confederate dead.

It was not the town's first cemetery—probably not the second. Before 1798 the churchyard of Christ's Church was the receiving ground for human remains. A yellow fever epidemic in 1798 filled up the real estate, however, and the churchwardens found themselves searching for new ground. It was found along Queen Street, very close to the old horse-racing track outside of town. Here in the midst of cedar trees Cedar Grove was founded and named.

Christ Church turned the cemetery over to the city in 1854; the city took a look at all the dogs, cattle and other creatures that freely wandered about the grounds and decided on its first major improvement: that same year a marl wall rose up around the grounds. The fine triple-arched "Weeping Gates" were installed as well and their $130 cost was donated by Dr. Francis L. Hawks, Episcopal historian and pastor

Against a daytime moon, an angel guards Cedar Grove.

and grandson of the palace-building John Hawks. Hawks—who earned that money from a lecture given in town—also dedicated the gateway, writing the poem that still appears in a marble plaque above the main arch:

> *Still hallowed be the spot where lies*
> *Each dear loved one in earths embrace,*
> *Our God their treasured duet doth prize,*
> *Man should protect their resting place.*

A walk through the cemetery is an education in tombstone design. Among the more interesting are "table top" graves, which feature marble tables that families used, occasionally, to literally dine with the dearly departed. Paper-thin old stones rise up in settled angles, white as chalk, while others are stained dark with age and moss, the names inscribed all but lost to the eroding effects of time. Everywhere, statuary abounds.

Poetry, philosophy and reminiscence abound, too. For instance, on the stone of Lucretia Jones (1780–1860): "To live in hearts we leave behind is not to die."

Naturally, much of the postmortem philosophy is of a distinctly Christian nature. A stone from 1870 suggests,

A marker showing the resting place of a Civil War veteran.

> *I would not live always: no—*
> *welcome the tomb*
> *Since Jesus hath lain there, I dread not its gloom*
> *There sweet be my rest till he bid me arise*
> *To hail him in triumph descending the skies.*

John Latham Gardner is memorialized after his death in 1869: "His last words were 'Jesus is precious to my soul He will take me to Glory.'"

Some are simple thoughts ("Loved one, farewell."), some bittersweet ("Just in the morning of his day, In youth and love, he died.") and some bitter ("The hope of the household is dead," written about a nineteen-year-old son killed in a hunting accident). Then there is the curiously cynical marker of John Jones:

> *Reflect O man while passing by*
> *As you are now so once was I.*
> *As I am now you soon will be:*
> *Prepare for death and follow me.*

Symbolic reliefs decorate many stones. Above, a weeping willow is an old symbol of the resurrection; the primitive face below represents the Angel of Death. The "pins" on either side of the stone symbolize the hinges of the gates of heaven.

The Confederate Memorial.

Stones to infants and preteens abound, testifying to the difficult life of America's past. One marker is a memorial to the losses of George and Leah Allen. Nine children, from a few months old to eleven years, are etched into the granite. The last five all died within a few days of each other in 1876.

Key to our interest, however, is Cedar Grove's service as a resting place for the Confederate dead. Though originally Unionist in sympathy, North Carolina reluctantly seceded from the Union in May of 1861; by the war's end it would send the most men to fight (125,000) of any Southern state—and lose the most (40,000) as well.

Numerous Confederate veterans (and casualties) lie in these grounds, from privates to generals (Major General Robert Ransom of the Twenty-fourth North Carolina is the highest-ranking Confederate on the grounds). It does not take long to find many of them. While most are marked with a simple designation of their service, at least one veteran, Captain E.M. Duguid of the Fifth North Carolina, was laid to rest with bragging rights: "A Survivor of the Lost cause, he was in most of the principal battles, Bull Run, Winchester, Yorktown, Sharpsburg, Gettysburg, the trenches at Petersburg. No braver man ever marched to the tap of drum, No man ever loved his land with greater love."

Captain Willis Roberts, who served with the Confederate States Navy, is there. In 1853 he sailed with Commodore Perry to open Japan; while there, he admired the native spider lilies and brought several bulbs back to New Bern, introducing the plant to America.

The centerpiece of the cemetery is the Confederate Memorial, under which the remains of most of the sixty-four Confederates who died in the Battle of New Bern are interred. The memorial itself— a Confederate soldier mounted atop a high spire—was dedicated in 1885, though its cornerstone was laid by the Ladies Memorial Association in 1866 (Confederate flags and banners were banned by the government during that event).

Of course, New Bern houses the Union dead as well—a trip a few blocks north on George Street (it turns into National Avenue) will bring you to the National Cemetery, housing Union remains on the left. You might want to make the visit by car, as it is several blocks away.

Walk east (toward the river) on Queen Street until you come to East Front Street. Turn right. Walk two or three blocks to the house (on the west side of the street) by the Rains brothers' historic marker. This is our next stop.

5. Rains Brothers House
605 East Front Street
Built circa 1810

This is one of New Bern's more recently moved (and most altered) houses, having been, just a few years back, firmly settled at 410 Johnson Street. It was built for one Gabriel Manigault Rains, who, according to nineteenth-century resident and historian Stephen F. Miller, "had the largest cabinet works in town." He had lived in New Bern since at least 1800, made his name and moved on to Alabama about 1838.

Mr. Rains employed a number of apprentices to work with him at his Middle Street shop. He had at least eight children as well, among them John, Gabriel and George. John developed the actor's bug and took to the boards with the town's Thespian Society. He must have been good—Miller remembered his "admirable" interpretation of Caleb Quotem, a "jack-of-all-trades" character well known in that day from George Colman's stock-performed farce, *The Review, or Wags of Windsor*.

Of greater import were the brothers George and Gabriel. Both would be West Point graduates and generals for the South in the Civil War.

George was the baby of the family, born in 1817. Like his brother, his fondness for chemicals would get him far in the world, but left his mother exasperated. "George is certainly one of the best of sons," she once said, "but I can't keep the boy decent; he burns up with his 'chemicals,' as he calls them, the best clothing I can have made for him."

George became president of a New York ironworks and got a number of patents for inventions relating to steam engines. When the war broke out he enlisted in the Confederate army. Possibly relying on his administrative skills and love of chemistry, George was put in charge of finding gunpowder for the munitions-starved South. He established powder mills in Augusta, Georgia, and managed to churn out 2,750,000 pounds of gunpowder. He was also in charge of collecting niter from Southern caves and developing the Nitre and Mining Bureau of the War Department. Following the war he settled in Augusta and taught chemistry at the Medical College of Georgia.

Gabriel was fourteen when George came into the world. This older brother was, like the younger, a tinkerer—his controversial invention would change the art of warfare around the world.

Joining the military after his 1827 graduation from West Point, Gabriel took part in the 1839 Seminole War. Harassed by Indians at Fort King, he jury-rigged a live shell, hiding it under a blanket near a pond where the Indians tended to get water. A Seminole set it off and several were killed. Encouraged, Gabriel tried again. When he checked it later, he found its explosion had done no harm. On his way back to the fort, his men were ambushed and he was so badly wounded that death notices were sent out.

In 1861 he resigned his commission and was named a brigadier general for the South. Commanding a force at Yorktown, he again began to play with mines, perfecting his old rendition, basing it upon a design by Samuel Colt. Designing it to lie underground, out of sight, he dubbed it a "torpedo" (although today we know them as land mines). He also developed a water version to sink ships. It was these that, in Mobile Bay, Admiral Farragut would damn while he went full speed ahead. After the war, Gabriel settled in South Carolina and continued to tinker with his deadly inventions (Miller would speak of a "peacemaker" weapon he was toying with).

The house itself is a Federal period house—very possibly in its original construction it was side-hall, with three bays instead of the present five. The dormers are Victorian additions, and the alteration of the first-floor windows to floor-length designs are also later additions. So you may have to squint quite hard to imagine the original building the Rains boys grew up in.

Walk to the next block (the corner of Johnson and East Front Streets). The tall brick house at this corner is our next tour; don't forget that this stop includes the kitchen house, located on East Front Street right behind the Slover House (which faces Johnson Street).

6. Charles Slover House and Kitchen
201 Johnson Street (House)
521 East Front Street (Kitchen)
Built circa 1848

Charles Slover House (right) and servants' quarters.

Here is a rare house on our tours, for it has neither been moved nor significantly altered. What you see is pretty much what was.

At the war's beginning, Charles Slover was one of the wealthiest men in town. He shared the house with a wife, eight children and ten slaves. The house's styling is Greek Revival, with columned entrance and every feature in perfect balance. So much so, in fact, that the central first-floor window on the East Front Street side of the house is permanently shuttered—this because it was put there to keep the exterior balance, despite the fact that a wall runs up the middle of the window inside.

Mr. Slover moved his family inland to High Point before New Bern's fall, not returning until the war's end. During the occupation the house became headquarters for General Ambrose Burnside and, later, General John Foster.

All this is interesting enough, but the most fascinating thing about the Slover House is its likely tie with literature—with Mark Twain. One

The Slover House served as headquarters for General J.G. Foster during the occupation. General Foster is at center, standing slightly in front of the other men. *Courtesy of Massachusetts MOLLUS Photograph Collection, U.S. Military History Institute, Carlisle Barracks, Pennsylvania.*

of Mark Twain's finest stories was not fictional at all. Titled "A True Story, Repeated Word for Word as I Heard It," it was first published in *Atlantic* magazine and later appeared in the collection *Sketches New and Old*. Both touching and harrowing, it was the reminiscences of a servant woman named "Auntie Cord" (in the story he changed her name to Aunt Rachel).

Auntie Mary Cord, an endlessly cheerful cook at Quarry Farm, where Twain and his family often visited, had been a slave most of her life. Twain asked her one evening, "How is it that you've lived sixty years and never had any trouble?"

"She turned her face over her shoulder toward me," Twain related, "and said, without even a smile in her voice: 'Misto Clemens, is you in 'arnest?…I's gwyne to tell you, den I leave it to you.'"

The story must be read to be fully appreciated, but here is the gist:

Raised in Virginia, Aunt Mary was forced to watch, in 1852, as her husband and seven children were sold at auction. "Dey put chains on us an' put us on a stan' as high as dis po'ch—twenty foot high—an' all de people stood aroun', crowds an' crowds," she said. "Dey sole my ole man, an' took him away, an' dey begin to sell my chil'en an take *dem* away, an' I begin to cry…when de las' one was gone but my little Henry, I grab' *him* clost up…an' I says; 'I'll kill de man dat tetches him!'"

Little Henry was sold, promising he would escape. Aunt Mary herself was sold to a New Bern man who was a colonel in the Confederate army. Upon the city's fall, Aunt Mary found herself suddenly free. She went to work as a cook in a "mons'us big house" for "de big Union officers…the biggest dey *is*." As the Slover House is "mons'us big" and as it contained the "biggest" officers, this makes it very likely that here is where Aunt Mary found herself (the Stanly House is also a possible setting for this story).

One day Aunt Mary was feeling particularly ornery—soldiers were dancing around in her kitchen ("My place was wid de officers, an' it

Vincent Colyer's 1864 sketch of a freed female slave. "Aunt Rachel" could have dressed very like this. *Etching from* Report of the Services Rendered to the Freed People, *Vincent Colyer, 1864.*

rasp me to have dem common sojers cavortin' roun'," she explains). One colored regiment in particular made a show that left her "a-bilin!" As one soldier came dancing along with a mulatto girl, she let them have it with both barrels of her tongue. "I wa'n't bawn in de mash to be fool' by trash!" she roared—a favorite phrase of hers. The words caused the young man to freeze. He wandered off, strangely thoughtful, but returned the next morning, coming up and staring hard into her face. It was then that Aunt Mary realized who this young soldier was—her Henry.

"Oh no, Misto C——" she concludes the story, "*I* hain't had no trouble. An' no *joy!*"

Behind the Slover House, on East Front Street, is a small home that was the kitchen and servants' quarters. Although Slover House also has a basement kitchen, it is quite possible that Aunt Mary's reunion took place in this building. Perhaps, as the head cook, she slept upstairs.

Both houses are currently owned by the same family, and are private residences.

Walk up Johnson Street (westward) to Craven Street, and turn left. About two-thirds of a block down (where Change Street "Y"s on to Craven) you will find our seventh stop.

7. Smith-Whitford House
506 Craven Street
Built circa 1772–82

This is the kind of house you might imagine seeing as the centerpiece in some movie with a Victorian setting. With its gingerbread porch trim, low picket fence and beautiful little gardens, its columned doorway and neat, elegant gables with arched windows, it is one of the most charming homes in town.

It was built for Henry Smith, who turned around and sold it for £10,000 to one Thomas Webber. Webber sold it a few years later, and

on it went from owner to owner until it finally landed in the hands of the Whitford family in 1875. Under this curious family the house was extensively remodeled with many fine Victorian flourishes. It is the Whitford family that lands this house in this tour—even though they did not purchase it until well after the war.

Mr. Whitford's house as seen from the southern approach.

John D. Whitford was a definite town "character"—opinionated, crusty, obsessed with the "Protestant work ethic" and throughout his life serving as embattled mayor, churchman, Confederate warrior and, finally, town historian whose rambling, meandering manuscript makes for some fascinating glances into the other townsmen of his time.

Whitford was born in 1825. His grandfather was Elijah Clark, a key founder of the First Baptist Church. Throughout his life Whitford took his Baptist faith to heart—he railed repeatedly in his writings about a group of Baptists who, in the 1740s, had asked North Carolina's colonial assembly for permission to build a church and got thrown in jail and publicly whipped for their efforts.

By his twenty-first year, Whitford was mayor of the town. New Bern had just taken over Cedar Grove Cemetery and, seeing the tendency of goats and cattle to graze among the stones (and, doubtless, to leave their "pies" in inappropriate places), he led a battle to have the cemetery enclosed by its present wall.

In 1854—at age twenty-nine—Whitford was elected president of the newly formed Atlantic and North Carolina Railroad. Bringing the all-important railroad into town, he connected New Bern to Beaufort and Goldsboro. When the war came rumbling along eight years later, these rails carried citizens and badly outnumbered Confederate soldiers to Kinston; but the victorious Yankees would make good use of the line for their own cause.

Whitford began his military interests early, joining the New Bern Light Infantry (militia units were not unknown during the mid-1800s), impressing his fellow members enough that, in 1859, they presented him with a silver pitcher.

In 1861 he represented the town at the state convention that elected to secede from the Union. Then, being a devout believer in action over words, he signed up to fight—his Whitford's Battalion of North Carolina Partisan Rangers would become the Sixty-seventh North Carolina Regiment. He defended his beloved town in the Battle of New Bern in March of 1862 under General Lawrence Branch. His regiment saw ongoing action around Kinston and later returned with General Robert F. Hoke in an attempt to retake New Bern in April 1864.

In addition to banging away at Yankees in the woods and swamps, Whitford was also the state agent for purchasing cavalry and other military supplies—a job he did so well that he received a letter of commendation from Robert E. Lee.

Whitford returned to his defeated town a hero, to a home that had been sacked. In his own words,

> [Mrs. Clark's] sister was left in charge of the writers house when he left New Bern in the Civil War, and as not entirely unexpected, she was summarily driven from it and the contents of each room appropriated for the use of those assuming charge, from the commanding officer down to

The Whitford house boasts one of the town's fine gardens.

the private, and were so finally carried off which was no exception to course pursued with the property of others in the town in like situation.

In 1866 Whitford was elected president of the railroad again. He was also elected (in a landslide) as a state representative in 1865. His ongoing service to his town would include such serious matters as service work with the Masons, directing the North Carolina Masonic Mutual Life Insurance Company and working for improvement of the Neuse River; and also in more frivolous and honorary functions, such as managing a traveling city baseball team and overseeing a postwar competition between former Yankees and former Rebs at the fairgrounds (the South rose again and won).

After the war, Whitford harbored little bitterness toward his former foes. He regretted slavery, but shared the popular opinion among whites that a good black man was one who "knew his place." He suggested that Baptists had suffered more greatly in America than had the slaves. Still, in his history, he often complimented various black citizens in the town.

His greatest legacy was his manuscript, *The Home Story of a Walking Stick—Early History of the Baptist Church at New Bern, N.C.* Though it purports to be a history of the church, the text actually covers about any history you could care to learn, from Graffenried's founding to Whitford's present (1900) day. Though his "facts" regarding the colonial period are strongly suspect, it is still a good way to learn about the character and events of the town in the nineteenth century. Many of his salty comments about churchgoers and town slackers are quite humorous—and startlingly modern.

Now for a little walking. Continue along Craven Street, heading toward the downtown. You will cross Broad Street and Pollock Street (the city hall is on your right). About halfway down the next block, our eighth stop awaits on the river side of the street.

8. Isaac Taylor House
228 Craven Street
Built circa 1792

Mr. Taylor's home and counting house was constructed as one of the town's earliest Federal side-hall buildings. It rises like a vertical monolith, the granddaddy of Craven Street houses.

Its builder—an ancestor of singer James Taylor—was a wealthy merchant, ship owner and planter who spoke in a Scottish brogue and

Members of the Forty-fourth Massachusetts Volunteer Militia pose outside their provost headquarters in 1863. *Courtesy of Paul Switzer.*

regularly met with God at the Presbyterian church. His wife inherited the estate in 1841 (along with a plantation and seventy-five slaves); she left it in turn to their spinster daughters, who briefly lost it to occupying forces.

Isaac Taylor, whom Stephen Miller would describe as a greatly respected elderly gentleman, purchased the lot in 1792 and built his home shortly after, probably hiring New Bern architect William Nichols. He ordered his house made of brick with walls two feet thick to protect against the fires that were so common in those days, and also to give the town a mansion to at least hold a candle to the only other brick home in town—the rapidly deteriorating Tryon Palace. The original building included a stable, outdoor kitchen and smokehouse. A fine ballroom was added to the second floor so that Mr. Taylor could keep his house as a social center in the town. It features unique Federal architecture.

Originally there were two front entrances—the one that is there now, which opened into the residence, and another one on the north side of the Craven Street façade, which opened into his counting office. There was no interior passage between the counting room and his residence at the time, which was typical. Perhaps there was too much concern of servants with quick fingers. If you look closely at the left, first-floor window as you stand before the house, you can still see the "ghost" of that second door.

Upon Isaac's death, his wife Hannah remodeled, removing the door and installing an interior passage. She then decorated the room in Greek Revival style—it is the only room with such molding today. She passed away in 1853. The place was left to their three spinster daughters (there were three others—among them Janet, who married the merchant William Hollister—we have met her before). Their names were Phoebe, Frances and Catherine.

The three ladies must have been horrified to see their fine mansion turned into a headquarters for regiments on provost duty. One of those regiments was the Forty-fifth Massachusetts, a nine-months regiment primarily recruited in Boston and made up of local elites. Albert W. Mann mentions the home in the regimental history:

> *Our regimental headquarters were on the east side of Craven Street, halfway between South Front and Pollock Streets in a three-story brick house, with one room and doorway on the street. Colonel Codman said it belonged to a family of aged maiden ladies, who fled when the city was taken, and left behind them quite a fine library of old English books.*

Apparently the boys took good care of the place, for on their heels their good friends, the Forty-fourth Massachusetts, took over the house for their turn at provost duty. Wrote Corporal James Gardner, "Each company had one or more houses allotted to its use, and among them were some of the pleasantest residences in the city. The Forty-fifth had left them in good condition, decorated them prettily, and many little

Was this pulley used as a means of supplying the Taylor sisters, who refused to come down the stairs during the occupation?

tokens of welcome greeted our arrival."

The story told today is that those "aged maidens" moved to the third floor when the soldiers arrived and refused to leave—that they even had their food and other needs brought up by a pulley that is still attached to the house. If so, Mr. Mann must have forgotten, and Mr. Gardner made no mention at all of such a curious situation. Still, a picture of 1863, with officers of the Forty-fifth posing before the house, definitely shows a mysterious woman peering out of a top-floor window.

It is possible the daughters were gone when these two regiments were stationed, but returned shortly after. But whether they camped upstairs or fled the city, the ladies regained their ownership rights in July of 1864, after they signed a statement of loyalty to the Union.

The Isaac Taylor house was modernized in 1900 with plumbing and electricity. At the same time, many of its outbuildings, no longer in use, were demolished. By 1940 it was deteriorating and being considered for demolition, when Mrs. Carrie Ward purchased and restored it, adding a radial brick patio in back and an antique side gate, purchased in Charleston. Sometime during the late 1950s or early 1960s a bomb shelter was installed in the basement. A recent owner, Paul Switzer, found it still well stocked with food from its date of origin, as well as six beds, weapons, a waste disposal system and radiation detectors.

The home is a fine reminder of the more mundane side of a soldier's life, of the struggles of families taken over by war and of New Bern's rich seafaring past.

From here, continue south on Craven. At the next intersection (South Front Street), looking to your left, you will see a tall, white-painted brick house on the south side of the street. This is our next stop.

9. Harvey Mansion
221 South Front Street
Built circa 1797–1804

Harvey Mansion as it stands today.

Here is another of those houses that has served, from its construction to the present date, a cornucopia of purposes: home, provost headquarters, barracks, boardinghouse, college and, finally, a restaurant and bed-and-breakfast.

At nine thousand square feet, this Adams-style mansion is one of the largest in town, built for the multiple purposes of residence and storehouse by its original builder, the English ship owner and merchant John Harvey. Among the men raising the house, we are told, was a middle-aged, Scottish immigrant named Robert Hay, whose home we visited in the "Colonial–Antebellum" tour.

Harvey purchased this lot in 1797 and built his home (which was also his warehouse and counting room) so large that he had to put an arched alleyway through the middle of it to access his Trent River wharves. During the Civil War, one of its occupiers, Henry Clapp of the Forty-fourth Massachusetts, described the building as it then stood: "It is a curious old brick house—built in the antique French fashion with an arch way running under it exactly in the middle, a door on either hand and an enclosure, once a court yard, behind."

Mr. Harvey died in 1828, full of years and money; the house remained in family hands until 1870. It is a Federal-style building of extremely simple lines, done in Flemish-bond brick with three floors, a full basement and an unfinished attic. In its original construction, the western portion was probably used as the warehouse.

We have a fair amount of commentary of the building's use during the Civil War, thanks to the letters of Henry Clapp. During much of its stay, the Forty-fourth Massachusetts spent its time in a row of leaky barracks along the river, where they spent time not on the march putting together amateur theatrical performances and balls (some of the men dressed the parts of women for such mock-solemn occasions) and marveling at the copperheads that dwelt in the swamps that bordered their site. After a number of quick campaigns, the soldiers pulled provost duty in the town. As a rule, this was not a favorite time for soldiers. Duty was more wearisome and they were forced to be more formal in their dress—not to mention the added time they would be snapping salutes to every officer who came their way.

The one upside of provost duty came in their new barracks. For convenience, the various companies were housed in the abandoned mansions of secessionists; often they not only enjoyed better buildings, but finer furnishings as well.

Henry Clapp, of Company F, boasted in a letter home,

The fireplace in the ballroom, now an elegant dining room in the Harvey Mansion restaurant.

I am quartered in the very pleasantest room in our building…Our room runs the whole length of the building, so that we have windows at each end. In front of our windows there are beautiful trees and from our back windows, we look out on the river and the shipping—a charming view. The room is three times as large as our parlor. Our bunks are made of wooden side pieces covered with canvass and are exquisitely comfortable— luxurious, indeed, after what we have been sleeping on.

Clapp's room was probably one of the warehouse portions of the place. Later, he wrote, "Last night Tim and I slept on a splendid bedstead with mattrases [*sic*]. The bedstead was of mahogany (veneered) with a great high piece at the head and must cost

Harvey House as it stood about the turn of the century (note the entryway door, now removed). *Courtesy of North Carolina Division of Archives.*

more than a hundred dollars. We have a marble topped table and ditto bureau with a fine mirror. In short we are in state."

Shortly after the war the Harvey Mansion changed hands and began its evolution of purpose, disrepair and renovation until, today, it is significantly different from the building Henry Clapp described. In 1898 it was converted into the Elm City Boarding House; then in 1904 it became the New Bern Military Academy. The mansion was converted into apartments for Cherry Point during World War II, and then served as the first site for Craven Technical Institute, which would become Craven Community College.

In 1974 the house was in such disrepair that the city attempted to have it torn down, but the keeper of the National Register refused to allow the historic building's destruction. Since 1980 it has served, under various owners, as a restaurant and, most recently, a bed-and-breakfast. Its dining rooms are on the second floor, where a grand ballroom was originally constructed. Harvey Mansion was recently described as New Bern's "most upscale restaurant" in the January 25 edition of the *New York Times*. Travel writer Nancy Bearden Henderson declared her meal here as "delectable."

For our last stop, we will turn from the Harvey Mansion and walk west on South Front Street. At Hancock Street (two or three concrete bears are here, in the form of seats, and the Antique Market, with a large mural, is on the corner), turn right. Go one block to the intersection of Hancock and Pollock Streets. Here is our final house on the Civil War tour.

10. Edward R. Stanly House
502 Pollock Street
Built circa 1848

The Ed Stanly House served as headquarters for the First Brigade, First Division, Eighteenth Army Corps during the occupation. *Courtesy of Massachusetts MOLLUS Photograph Collection, U.S. Military History Institute, Carlisle Barracks, Pennsylvania.*

It is a curious box on the corner, made more curious these days by alabaster-colored modern sculptures in the side yard. With floor-length first-floor windows and an attic lined with windows just about wide enough to serve as horizontal arrow slits, the whole house looks bottom-heavy. It so resembles an old decorative tin box that, if it weren't for the spray of colorful pots and flowers and the fine little entrance portico, you would almost expect to open the door and find giant saltine crackers inside.

It is cuter—and just as curious—as it sounds. This is the house that Edward R. Stanly built, a side-hall monument to Greek Revivalism.

He's not the same Ed Stanly who came tramping home at Lincoln's behest to be military governor in town. So far as we know, he was no relation to the Stanly dynasty at all. But he was successful in his own right. Born in Jones County in 1816, Stanly arrived in New Bern about 1839, married Elizabeth Tull and settled down. He was a manufacturer whose worth, in 1850, was $10,000. He built Stanly Hall downtown in 1874, just a couple of years before he retired from his work and moved out of town.

Stanly was a respected community member who was an original director with the Atlantic and North Carolina Railroad. We do not know if he stayed in town during the Civil War; if he did, he probably took a fair amount of ribbing for sharing the unpopular military governor's name.

Also, if he stayed, he was displaced, for his house was taken over as headquarters for the First Division, First Brigade, Eighteenth Army Corps, which was commanded by General Innis Palmer. The picture on the previous page was taken in 1864, when the house served as said headquarters. In September and October of that year a yellow fever epidemic swept

Detail of the entryway shows a change from simple Doric square columns to a more ornate style.

New Bern, killing dozens of people, residents as well as occupation forces. The medical corps should have fought the epidemic by enthusiastically swatting mosquitoes; instead, they burned barrels of pitch to blacken the sky with smoke and burned down several warehouses that, they suspected, were keeping the miasmic waters of a recent downpour from properly draining. Among the fever's victims was a young lieutenant from this headquarters home.

The house, today, maintains much of its original shape. Among the most obvious changes, as you can see by comparing the 1864 picture with the entryway detail, is the replacement of the simple square columns with a set of more elaborate design.

The house now serves as the office for an architectural firm.

Returning to your car is an easy walk. Head west on Pollock Street. Just a couple of houses (and a high chain-link fence) will bring you back to the historical society, where we began.

Like many historic houses in New Bern, the owners pay close attention to flower gardens (as shown). This one also has a sculpture garden in the side yard.

NEUSE RIVER

JOHNSON ST.

CHANGE ST.

LINDEN ST.

NEW ST.

GEORGE ST.

BROAD ST.

POLLOCK ST.

HANCOCK ST.

MIDDLE ST.

CHRIST CHURCH

CRAVEN ST.

EAST FRONT ST.

TRENT RIVER

The Gilded Age—and Beyond

I t appears in a *Morning New Bernian* advertisement of 1916 and catches the fast-talking fever of that age. A boss, noticing that the oppressive Southern heat has left his office workers lethargic, demands an office boy get a case of Pepsi. "Don't you understand me?" he shouts. "A dozen bottles of this new high-speed drink. This pure juice-of-the fruit Stuff that makes you so glad there's work to do, you soon have it done and are out looking for more!"

Then and now: A view of New Bern from the Trent River railroad bridge in 1895 and 2007. The steeple of Christ Church, visible in the older picture, is hidden by hotels today. *1895 picture courtesy of North Carolina Division of Archives.*

An old view of East Front Street, taken near the present-day Sudan Temple looking north. *Courtesy of Stith and Stith Pa.*

Contrary to occasional belief, Southern history does not end with Appomattox Court House. Though financially devastated by the war, New Bern would continue to exist—and hit some boom times. New Bern—and, of course, the state—went through Federal occupation and Reconstruction for two years (1867–68). This was not an entirely unfriendly event. Sometimes the two "sides" would intermarry or face off in friendly sports competitions.

Turpentine continued to be an important industry, but it was another product of trees—namely the trees themselves—that returned New Bern to prosperity. Cypress, pine, oak and other woods fed sixteen lumber mills by 1916. Three were owned by William Blades, whose mansion's opulence outshone anything in New Bern. Other growing businesses included the seafood industry.

World War II brought more prosperity: the newly opened Cherry Point Marine Corps air base brought soldiers into town seeking housing and R and R. Wooden minesweepers were built for the war effort. The Barbour Boat Works launched its first minesweeper in 1942.

Crabbing has been a way of life in New Bern for many years.

One of New Bern's most trumpeted achievements was the invention of Pepsi-Cola in 1898. Originally known as Brad's Drink, it was invented by local pharmacist Caleb Bradham and first made and served in a humble drugstore. Bradham soon fitted out a factory to produce it.

Coffeehouse of the turn of the century. Caleb Bradham and acquaintances gather at the soda fountain at his downtown pharmacy about 1908. *Courtesy of New Bern Historical Society*.

Not all things went well: in December 1920, New Bern experienced its most devastating fire, which destroyed a large section of town, including a church, a lumberyard and numerous small businesses. Affecting mainly the black district, it resulted in many of New Bern's African American citizens migrating out of the area.

For a time following the war, New Bern faced a crisis. Many of its businesses were moving out; the downtown was deteriorating. However, a dream to recreate Tryon Palace began to infect a number of people. Its eventual reconstruction helped guide New Bern to rediscovering her historical roots and building the tourist trade that is now so much a part of her personality. The Tryon Palace Commission was set up by

In 1904 Caleb Bradham purchased the Bishop Factory at Johnson and Hancock Streets, converting it into the first Pepsi-Cola factory. By 1910 it was producing 1,200 gallons of syrup an hour. *Courtesy of Pepsi-Cola Bottling Company, New Bern*.

the state legislature in 1945. Although a street ran right through the middle of the palace's buried remains and numerous houses filled the grounds, the commission raised funds and purchased the land, cleared or moved the buildings and painstakingly rebuilt the palace to its original plans. Rising from her ashes, this structural phoenix opened to the public in 1959.

Historic preservation and community revitalization are now key elements of New Bern's growth—along with the

Above: A mill tower on the north side of town rises over the Neuse River's morning mist.

Left: Lovingly kept flower gardens have been an added bonus to walks around historic New Bern throughout its history.

Below: Branches frame a boat on the Neuse. In the background you can see the city hall clock tower, Christ Church steeple and the gold Sudan Temple dome.

continuing development of strong industries such as Maola Dairy, Weyerhauser and BSH Bosch and Hatteras Yachts.

You can still find boats lining wharves in New Bern, but they carry pleasure sailors, not fish or goods. New Bern has not been the capital or— outside of Craven County— the center of political power in the state for 150 years. But she has found her roots and, yet again, vitality. This tour looks at the homes of some of the people and businesses that helped bring that about.

New Bern is host to several parades. Every January, it hosts the regional Shriner parade.

We start at the corner of Pollock and Middle Streets. Stand by the wrought-iron fence of Christ Church and look west: that dominating business building across the street is our first stop.

1. The Elks Temple
400 Pollock Street
Built 1908

It is New Bern's largest business building and one of its oldest and finest, raising its five stories of yellow brick and terra cotta trimmings at the corner of Pollock and Middle Streets. It was constructed by some of New Bern's richest men at the turn of the century and featured plush meeting spaces, department stores and offices for every kind of business.

The Elks Building is the largest business office in New Bern.

Now, unfortunately, it stands empty, and for several years its fate—whether restoration or ruin—has been unknown. Happily, its current owners, Applegate Architecture, feel they will definitely be able to sell the structure to investors who will restore the place to new days of glory.

The turn of the century was a boom time in New Bern: several fine mansions grew up from the streets and numerous businesses, such as the Gaston Hotel, were renovated or begun. The headquarters of the New Bern Elks Lodge 754, this fine edifice was financially backed by some of New Bern's wealthiest businessmen, among them the Blades brothers James, William and Charles.

A souvenir bicentennial (1910) booklet about New Bern businesses describes this then-brand-new business:

The Elks' Temple, a new 5-story, yellow brick building, completed just a year ago by the Elk's Construction Co., local capitalists, contains a large department store, office rooms and public library, with the Elk's lodge and club rooms on the 5th floor, the latter being unquestionably the handsomest furnished lodge and club rooms in the entire South. The views of the harbor and surrounding country from the

Detail work on the Elks Building.

lofty club rooms, excite the admiration of all who visit the city. A party of Rhode Island veterans…were most agreeably impressed with the marked improvements found on every hand. This building, furnished complete cost about $120,000. The Elk's Lodge here has a membership of 225 who are the representative business men of the city.

The ground floor was used as storefront, housing several businesses including J.J. Baxter's department store, which featured clothing, dry goods, shoes, trunks, furnishings and millinery. The second, third and fourth floors were office spaces. Among the inhabitants were Ward & Allen Attorneys and Dr. Z.V. Parker, dentist.

The top floor was an elaborate meeting space for the Elks and their guests. The Masons, Woodmen, Odd Fellows, Knights of Pythias, the Red Men and the Royal Arcanum also had branches here, according to *Illustrated City of New Bern.*

This building is decorated in a style known as Beaux Arts, a kind of classical style, including its arched windows on the Pollock Street first floor and the fluted columns of its main entrance on the same street. At one time, its most prominent feature was an elk's head overlooking the city from its fifth-floor street corner.

Turn and walk down Pollock Street toward the river. City hall is our next stop; it is on your left at the next corner

The Elks Building in its heyday. *Courtesy of Stith and Stith Pa.*

(Pollock and Craven). With all its color and those bears sticking out of the walls, it is hard to miss.

2. New Bern City Hall
Corner of Pollock and Craven Streets
Built circa 1895–97. Extensive remodeling circa 1904.

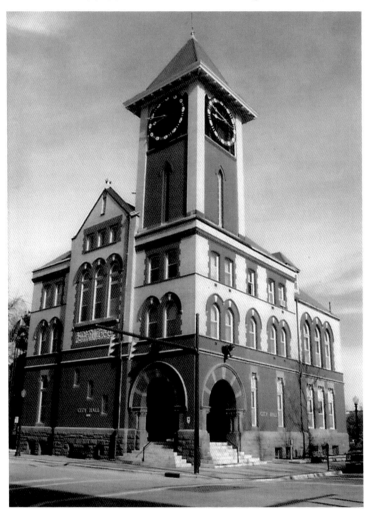

If there is any building in town that seems to shout New Bern's connection with its namesake in Switzerland, it is city hall.

This curious collection of styles, quaintness and colorful construction did not start life as a city building. At first it served as a combination post office, federal courthouse and customhouse. City hall at that time was on Craven Street, a block north.

Congress approved the building's construction in 1889 and plans were completed by 1894. The original building was completed at a price of $68,756.60, using brownstone quarried in Sanford, North Carolina, along with red pressed brick on the first floor and yellow brick above (with red brick detailing). A fine relief featuring foliate work and shield decorates the central, two-story windows on the Pollock Street side.

But residents complained that there was no clock by which to set their timepieces. So in 1908, a New Bern congressman, Charles R. Thomas, garnered his constituents' favor by securing a Seth Thomas illuminated, four-faced clock (at this writing, its 2,800-pound inner works are being removed for repair in time for the 2010 tricentennial, after which they will be displayed to the public). The clock was installed in 1911 and ran until 1999, when mechanical problems prompted the city to install a digital/electrical system to run it.

In 1935, the city took over the federal courthouse, turning its second-floor courtroom into

Above: City hall in 1896 (it was a federal building then). The clock would not be added until 1909. *Courtesy of North Carolina Division of Archives.*

Below: Detail of a flag given to New Bern by the Bern (Switzerland) aldermen.

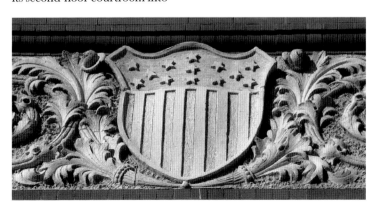

Detail of relief work on city hall's Pollock Street wall.

the official meeting hall. A year later, two brass bears were taken down from the old city hall and remounted. They now dangle over the entryway at the corner of Pollock and Craven Streets, and each bear has a name—the one over Pollock Street is King William II, named after the New Bern lumber baron William B. Blades; and the one over Craven Street is Prince Albert, named after the town's mayor and alderman over many years.

Inside, much of the building's original decoration remains—interspersed with some very modern additions. The Victorian stairwells are especially fine to examine. Inside the meeting hall a number of artifacts are on display, including the original flag given to the town by the residents of Bern, Switzerland, in 1896.

Visitors are welcome during visiting hours; you can feel free to browse the interior and view the courtroom and its artifacts for yourself.

Cross the street at the intersection and then turn right down Craven Street. A few buildings down you will see our next destination on the left.

3. Stephen's Brick Block
Old City Hall
220–226 Craven Street
Built circa 1817

This old Federal-style structure is a chameleon in New Bern's history. It started as a business—making it the oldest mercantile structure in town—then became a fire station, then city hall and finally has come full circle as a place to shop.

It was built by Marcus Cicero Stephens, who apparently had a difficult time finding renters. He mortgaged the property to the bank in 1827, which sold it as four separate units to businessmen. Its most interesting occupiers appeared after the Civil War in the form of the Atlantic Steam Fire Engine Company.

The first modern fire department in town, the Atlantic Fire and Hook and Ladder Company was founded in 1845. During the Civil War, most of its members had gone to fight. In January 1865, another fire company

Old city hall and the Atlantic Pump Company about 1900. *Courtesy North Carolina Division of Archives.*

started up in competition—this one, the New Bern Steam Fire Engine Company No. 1, by Yankee soldiers who'd decided to make New Bern their permanent home. The two fire companies became fierce competitors. It wasn't long before citizens were more concerned with which company made it first to a fire than whose house was burning down.

In the early days, firemen had their work cut out for them—not only did they have to battle often-hopeless blazes, but they also had to drag their pump engines by hand to the conflagrations. Then they connected their pump to a well or river (whichever was closest) and every available man would start pumping to get the pressure to run the hose.

In 1879—a few years before the company occupied Stephens's former business— the Atlantic Fire and Hook and Ladder Company received a new steam-operated fire engine. The New Bern company one-upped its rival by obtaining a Button Steam Fire Engine (thus earning themselves the moniker of "The Button Company"). Other fire companies eventually cropped up (including the black-run Kimball Fire Company), but these two remained the giants, struggling for recognition as the number one company in town.

By 1888, the City of New Bern purchased the entire complex, turning it into city

Having started as a business, old city hall has served as a fire department, government building and finally returned to its roots.

hall, but still sharing it with Atlantic Fire and Hook and Ladder. A brick façade was put up about 1895. Then, in 1914, the city purchased three copper Bern-style bears—mouths open, red tongues curling—to mount on the building at a cost of seventy-five dollars each. In about 1915, cast-iron light fixtures—much resembling the pawn shop symbol—were mounted; they are still there as well.

In 1936, city hall was moved to the old Federal Building at the corner of Pollock and Craven Streets—its current location. The bears moved with the city fathers—two of them to the new courthouse digs and the third to the Broad Street fire station.

In more recent days the building has returned to its mercantile roots, serving the community as a collection of interesting shops.

If you would like to learn more about old city hall's past as a fire station, a visit to the New Bern Fireman's Museum at 408 Hancock Street is a good idea. Along with information, it includes the Atlantic Hook and Fire and Ladder Company's 1879 pumper and the competing "Button Company's" button pumper. You can contact them at (252) 636-4087.

Now it's time for a little exercise. Turn around and head back up Craven Street, past the new city hall and on up to Broad Street. Cross over and turn right, walking toward the river, past the Sudan Shrine Temple. At the circle you will turn left (onto East Front Street). Just beyond the Sudan parking lot on the left, you will see the next home.

4. The Jesse S. Claypoole House
411 East Front Street
Built 1925

Without this house, there would be no *Wall Street Journal*. Well, at least it's nice to think that way.

It is a mixture of architectural styles, including Colonial Revival, and was built for insurance man Jesse S. Claypoole. Its lunette attic windows have reminded more than one person of that famous house in *Amityville Horror*—though there are no ghost stories, benign or horrific, associated here. We include the house not only for its charm, but also for the charming story and brush with fame that it entails.

Jesse and his wife Bonnie had a daughter named Frances, who in 1931 had just turned sixteen and was about to meet one of America's great men of the press.

Not too far away, in Chapel Hill, there lived a seventeen-year-old man with the curious name of Vermont Connecticut Royster (1914–1996). It was his grandfather's name, whose siblings were also named after states. Iowa, Michigan and Oregon were among the elder Vermont's brothers, and his sisters included Louisiana, Virginia and Georgia.

The younger Royster and some friends had decided to visit New Bern—even then a resort town—to celebrate the Fourth of July. Later

Vermont Connecticut Royster, who would lead the *Wall Street Journal* to national prominence, found his bride in this 1925 New Bern home.

he would recall "a beautiful waterfront, there at the confluence of the Neuse and Trent, and there was a charm to the streets with their old houses, their old buildings."

He was, in his own words, "a stripling youth, doing the things the young men did in those days—swimming on the beach at Morehead, watching all the girls go by, chasing them when we could at dances, or furtively courting them on darkened front porches." Royster would never forget the ladies—in a speech to the New Bern Preservation Foundation that he gave in 1973, he recited many of the ladies' names by heart. The most memorable girl he met at those dances was Frances, who "above all became entwined in my life."

Royster and Frances dated for several years, so doubtless he came to know the Claypoole home quite well. Sometime later, Royster graduated from the University of North Carolina at Chapel Hill, majoring in classical languages—which was not exactly a skill in high demand. Still, with the experience of editing his college paper and a lot of chutzpah, he showed up at the editorial offices of the *Wall Street Journal* and convinced them to hire him on as a reporter in 1936. The following year, on June 5, he and Frances were married and, except for visits to the folks, their story in New Bern came to an end.

Vermont quickly built his career, becoming senior editor by 1951 and winning the Pulitzer Prize for editorial writing in 1953. He is credited with building the *Journal* into the recognized business paper leader that it is today.

It is a hopeful guess on our part that his love for Frances drove him to land that job so he could support his bride. True or not, he would always feel affection for North Carolina's second-oldest town: "It is especially for my Frances," he said in 1973, "that my heart is warmed by your kindness in this homecoming."

Now walk down East Front Street, just a couple of houses, to see our next home, again on the left.

5. Coor-Bishop House
501 East Front Street
Built circa 1770–78. Extensive remodeling circa 1904.

Here is a house that is loaded with history—much of it antebellum. We include it in this section because of its extensive 1904 remodeling work—done, of course, by Herbert Woodley Simpson.

James Coor constructed the original house, and had it facing New Street. John Hawks's closest competition, Coor built a number of homes in New Bern and dabbled quite a lot in real estate (his own home, the Gaston House, is covered in the "Colonial–Antebellum" tour). It is not easy to imagine what the place looked like when Coor was finished: Simpson's work has pretty much engulfed its original style.

The house went through several owners early on. Its most important early resident was George Pollock, who is described extensively in Stephen F. Miller's memoir of 1820, *New Bern Fifty Years Ago*. Pollock, he said, was one of the wealthiest men in the state, with "half a dozen plantations" and "some fifteen hundred slaves."

Pollock did not really live here. "Mr. Pollock passed his summers generally at Philadelphia and in Europe, and probably [was] in

Newbern but once a year for a short time after having inspected his plantations and their management," Miller wrote. He added that Pollock had the curious habit of insisting he had been knighted by the king of Great Britain. Whether he really was or not, he probably looked it: "He was a tall square-built man, of striking physiognomy, and was a fine specimen of Nature's nobility."

Pollock—who never married—entertained President James Monroe and Secretary of War John C. Calhoun in April 1819. The well-known New Bern statesman, John Stanly, was also a guest and gave a flowery toast in the president's honor.

Detail of the pedimented central dormer.

Money can't buy everything, and Mr. Pollock was an ill-fated fellow: he died at one of his plantations in 1839 when he was killed by his horse, which had reared up and fallen on him in the saddle.

Another owner of the house was Mathias E. Manly, a future judge in the State Supreme Court. The house stayed in the Manly family from 1847 until 1900, when Edward K. Bishop, wholesaler of lumber and groceries, bought it. Not satisfied with his house's appearance, perhaps envying Mr. Blades's over on Middle Street, Bishop got hold of Herbert Woodley Simpson and told him to redesign the whole place. He even had Simpson turn the house ninety degrees to face East Middle Street.

After extensive remodeling, Corinthian columns now hold up the porch.

What you see is Mr. Simpson's work. These include the fine porch with its Corinthian columns and the pedimented dormers sitting nobly on the roof. Extensive Colonial Revival modeling was done within as well.

Over the years the Coor-Bishop house has not only gone through a major face-lift directional change; the ground on which it sets has shrunk. Originally the lot covered the entire block. As the lot was broken up and sold, piecemeal, its two dependencies were also shifted about and became separate properties. These, which have stylistic details similar to the original master house, are at 213 Linden Street and 214 New Street.

Walk past the next three houses and you will come upon our next home on your left.

6. Larry I. Moore House
511 East Front Street
Built circa 1904

When you think of those cars full of red-fezzed men in the annual Shriner parade or of burned children being treated in Shriner hospitals, let this fine house come to mind. Its builder was one of the men who started the local Shriner Temple back in 1916.

Larry I. Moore had a lot just a couple of houses down from Mr. Bishop and his newly remodeled Coor-Bishop house. Perhaps the two got to talking; in any case, Moore contacted Bishop's architect (as did just about everyone else in those days) and told Mr. Simpson to design something similar for him.

It rose in 1908, and an older, Federal-period house was moved to a new location on Change Street to make room. The new mansion was a modern marvel. One cannot help but notice the huge Corinthian columns supporting a massive neoclassical portico and forming the focus of the broad veranda of this luxurious home. Smaller columns support separate porch roofs to either side, each in perfect balance in a neat, neoclassical style. Inside, the house is Colonial Revival.

A founder of the New Bern Shriners and the son of a Primitive Baptist elder, Larry Ichabod Moore had become a lawyer of great significance. At one time he was law partner with Charles Aycock (governor of North Carolina in 1901). As one of his main clients was the railroad, Moore elected to move to New Bern in 1907. He went into partnership with William Dunn Jr. and formed the law firm of Moore and Dunn. They kept four offices on the fourth floor of the Elks Building.

Moore's son, Larry Jr. (who lived in Wilson), served in the state legislature for twenty years, beginning in 1926. Here was a case of father following son, for Larry Sr. later ran for, and held, office in the State Senate in 1933. During his lifetime as a lawyer, he argued eighty-five cases before the North Carolina Supreme Court.

An active member at St. John's Masonic Lodge, he and a few others began to hanker to take Masonry to the next level—which was, of course, the Shriners, who would ultimately be housed in the Sudan Temple. Moore was the lodge's first high priest and prophet (A.B. Andrews was the potentate).

The stairwell as it appeared in 1910. *Courtesy North Carolina Division of Archives.*

The opening ceremonies for the Shrine club were quite a to-do in town. Hundreds of Shriners came by rail from Wilmington and Charlotte and were registered (and many housed) at the ritzy Gaston Hotel. A huge oyster roast fêted them at a local tobacco warehouse (the clean smell of raw tobacco must have been very fine), and a grand parade capped the day.

The Shriner celebration had its light moments. According to the *Morning New Bernian*, they gathered at the corner of Pollock and Middle Streets (where the cannon is upended in the ground) playing pranks "to make the life of all the Nobles perfectly miserable" before all interested citizenry. In one stunt a poor, portly fellow had to measure the length of a block using an eel. "Mr. Pope is rather a stout man and it was a little difficult for him to get up and down," the paper noted, "but it had to be done and eventually he announced the distance."

He probably didn't touch seafood delicacies for a year.

Our next—somewhat more modest—house is just a couple of doors down on the left, at the intersection of Change Street.

7. The Louisiana House
(Dawson-Clarke House)
519 East Front Street
Built circa 1807–10

Here is the abode of the daughters of the arts. This Federal-period house, with its broad and breezy two-story porch, was the home of both one of North Carolina's most talented female writers and her granddaughter, one of our finest photographers.

The house was originally built by Levi Dawson, of whom we know precious little. He was a representative in the North Carolina House of Commons in 1790. Through wills and sales it worked its way through owners until, in about 1870, it fell into the hands of Mary Bayard Clarke, who christened it with its curious name.

Clarke (1827–1886) had been born Mary Bayard Devereux in Raleigh, a descendant of the New England preacher Jonathan Edwards and North Carolina patriarch Thomas Pollock. While living on a Louisiana sugar plantation in 1848 she met and married New Bern resident William Clarke, an honored Mexican War major (he was severely wounded at the Battle of the National Bridge). The pair traveled, living in Raleigh, then Texas to benefit her somewhat consumptive health. During the Civil War, her husband took up the sword again, fighting with the Twenty-fourth North Carolina until a shell fragment shattered his shoulder at the battle below Drewry's Bluff in Virginia in May 1864. After a short stint at home to recuperate, he headed back for Virginia, was captured en route and sat out the rest of the war in a prison camp in Delaware.

Mary consoled herself by taking up the pen. Her talent was needed to fill the dwindling family coffers. Her patriotic verses were soon quoted across the South. Mary edited a book of her own and others' work, *Mosses from a Rolling Stone, or The Idle Moments of a Busy Woman*, and, in 1865, began editing a women's and agricultural magazine called *Southern Field and Fireside*. During the war, many of her verses honored the Rebel cause. As her life went on, she wrote book reviews, hymns, novelettes and a translation of Victor Hugo's poems.

In 1870 the Clarkes returned to New Bern and bought the Dawson-Clarke House. Mary called it the Louisiana House, apparently in honor of her days at the sugar plantation, and she lived there until her death.

Five years after Mary's arrival, a granddaughter was born in her home just in time for Christmas—December 17, 1875. The child was given the same first name as her mother and grandmother (Mary) and her grandmother's middle name (Bayard).

Mary Bayard Morgan started a professional career early in life. At seventeen, she was teaching at a deaf school in Arkansas and, in 1897 (when she was twenty-two) she was handling the same career in Georgia. There she married Charles Wootten, had two sons and found herself abandoned by 1901.

A single mother now, she returned to New Bern to find a way to support her boys. At first she turned to painting calendars, greeting cards and fans. Her wealthy neighbor, Caleb Bradham, knocked on her door and hired her to design the first logo for his famous drink, Pepsi-Cola, in 1902.

As a supplement to this rather meager income, Ms. Wootten took up a borrowed camera. She studied under a local photographer and discovered her new love of the magic of portraiture. Soon her work was appearing around the nation. She became so well known that, for a time, she even operated a studio in New York.

The uniqueness of her style was realism: she was one of the first professionals to photograph ordinary people at their work. Her shots are often carefully considered candids; in their stark realism they shine with special beauty.

Bayard Wootten (inset and standing in the river behind her camera) was New Bern's best-known photographer. *Courtesy North Carolina Division of Archives.*

Wootten became the first woman to take aerial photographs in 1914, when she climbed onto a Wright brothers' airplane and, in the air, aimed the camera between her feet to shoot views of New Bern and the Neuse River. By the late 1920s, Ms. Wootten had moved to Chapel Hill, where she remained for most of her life until her death in 1959. Her portraits were famous in North Carolina, and were shown in such cities as Charleston and Boston.

At one time, Wootten's studio stood on this lot on East Front Street, beside the house, until the 1950s. The house itself has survived its many restorations to maintain most of its original design and charm.

If you are interested in learning more about our Marys, you might purchase or borrow from your library *Live Your Own Life: The Family Papers of Mary Bayard Clarke*. On Mary Bayard Wootten, a fine book is Jerry W. Cotton's *Light and Air: The Photography of Bayard Wootten*.

Time to put on a little more mileage. Continue down East Front Street to Johnson Street and turn left. You will pass some very fine homes along this stretch. Keep an eye to your right: when you reach Middle Street (the library is across the way), you have reached the next home.

8. Blades Mansion
602 Middle Street
Built 1903

Babe Ruth slept here. For some folks, that's more exciting than learning that George Washington also found the place and tucked himself in.

It was in the 1930s, and the Babe was an avid duck hunter. Craven County was an area known for its preponderance of ducks, and

Sleigh riders admire the new mansion on a rare, snowy day in 1904. *Courtesy of the North Carolina Division of Archives.*

William Blades, known for his very fine mansion, was an acquaintance of the baseball great. So when Babe visited to depopulate the ducks, he put up with Blades for the night.

Blades was one of those "magnates" who was making New Bern a prosperous place at the turn of the century. Born a Marylander in 1854, he had started a lumber business with his brother James when New Bern—her forests, rails and labor force—sent him a siren song. In 1893 he incorporated the Blades Lumber Company in James City, along the Trent, and soon was operating additional sawmills on upper East Front Street, Bridgeton and over at Knobbs Creek.

In addition, William served as vice-president of the New Bern Banking and Trust Company (his brother James was president) and as city alderman from 1913 to 1917.

The Blades mansion reflects his wealth—and his love of wood. Herbert Woodley Simpson, the prominent architect who built Centenary Methodist and B'nai Sholem Temple, among other buildings and residences, was brought on board to raise this fine mansion. With its many turrets and gables, its profusion of round windows, porches and curved glass, it is a curious hodgepodge of Queen Anne and Colonial Revival styles.

Seeing it is like looking upon a fairytale. At the south corner is a round turret; at the north, a turret more or less octagonal, with a third-floor porch fit for Rapunzel and her endless hair. Numerous Corinthian columns support the broad porch roof (it extends along two streetfronts).

Inside are numerous rooms and fireplaces, covered with floors and intricately worked entryways of oak and other fine woods. Some of the interior, according to Sandbeck, is styled after the Federal-period

A cluster of turrets, peaks and chimneys at the Blades mansion.

lodge room at St. John's Masonic Lodge. During the Bladeses stay the home was a continual center of social life in New Bern.

It is possibly the grandest mansion and private home in the city, and gives an appropriate picture of the style and grandeur that lumber barons and railroad kings brought to the early twentieth-century town.

Turn back toward downtown, crossing over to the library side of the road and following Middle Street. Cross Broad Street (you will pass the Chelsea restaurant) and a few other businesses. Just past the Cow Café you will reach our next destination.

9. Bank of the Arts
The Peoples Bank
317 Middle Street
Built 1913

This nifty little financial institution (now an artistic institution), as small as it is, seizes your gaze as you pass down Middle Street. With its tall Ionic columns and Doric pilasters, it seems ready to spill Medea or Oedipus onto the streets.

It was built in 1913 by the Peoples Bank, a company founded six years before and boasting businessman William Dunn as president and Caleb D. Bradham, the Pepsi-Cola founder, as vice-president. Its architect was Wilmington's Burett H. Stephens, while the contractor who raised the walls was Harrison S. Hancock, the same company that built the Athens Theater on Pollock Street. Over the century, Eastern Bank & Trust and First Citizen's Bank and Trust also occupied the building.

Today the Peoples Bank still houses treasures—but these are treasures of clay, acrylic, watercolor and oil. The Craven Arts Council and Gallery was formed in the 1980s by the merger of the Craven Community Arts Council and the New Bern Art Gallery. First Citizens donated the building to be used as headquarters. It was simply logical to rechristen the place "Bank of the Arts."

While the exterior remains the same—with its huge arched window, bronze grillwork and quaint over-the-door clock—extensive remodeling has changed the inside. The large foyer makes a fine and impressive gallery for ongoing shows of both local and distant artists, while a walk through the old vault will bring you into a pleasant gift shop of local artisans' works. The gallery is open and free to the public from 10:00 a.m. to 6:00 p.m. daily. It is curious to stroll the room and try to imagine, from the hints left by doors and fixtures, how this place may have looked in its financial heyday.

Along with regular shows of artistic works in nearly all mediums, the Bank of the Arts also hosts cultural programs and music and serves as a sales center for tickets to local drama productions. Fundraisers are held—art auctions among them—for building improvements

Above: Once a bank for commerce, now this is a bank for the area's arts.

Right: The gallery holds ongoing arts shows. A gift shop is accessible through the old vault.

and upkeep. The gallery also oversees an outdoor display of modern sculpture on a lot at the corner of Broad and Middle Streets.

We wrap our tour by walking the rest of the block (you are now, again, in front of the Elks Building). Catty-corner across the street you will see our final destination. Feel free to step inside and have a cold drink while you take in the final tour stop!

10. Where Pepsi was Born: The Hughes Building
256 Middle Street
Built 1935–40

The birthplace of Pepsi. Sort of.

New Bern has been fortunate to maintain much of its history in the form of original buildings (though sometimes you have to hunt around to find out where those buildings have been moved). That is not, however, *always* the case.

Stand at the corner of Middle and Pollock Streets, looking east toward the river. The old Baxter building clock stands a few yards off, looking picturesque in its juxtaposition to the city hall; and right at the corner, under a tasteful blue awning, you will see a little store emblazoned as "The Birthplace of Pepsi." A bronze plaque honors it; a historic marker proudly boasts of "Brad's drink," later christened "Pepsi." And it's all true.

Except that this isn't the building. It's just the spot.

The building where pharmacist Caleb Bradham invented his flavorful drink in 1898 stands in memory more than fact; it was torn down in 1931 and replaced by this one, raised between 1935 and 1940. The present store, while seriously lacking in the powders, ointments and cigars of Caleb's little business, has a luxurious counter with an old-time looking soda fountain from which visitors can enjoy a glass of Pepsi or Mountain Dew. Around you, memorabilia abounds in souvenir license plates, T-shirts, key chains and other whatnots.

Caleb Bradham. *Courtesy North Carolina Division of Archives.*

How did Caleb come upon his decision to name Pepsi-Cola? The official answer is that it was named for one of its ingredients, pepsin, which was supposedly an aid in digestion. He no doubt came to the decision after purchasing, for one hundred dollars, the rights to the name of a defunct New Jersey drink, "Pep Cola."

There is a much more charming story floating around that Caleb really came upon his drink's name as he gazed across the street at Christ Episcopal Church and began to play with the name "Episcopal." "Pepsi-Cola" was the result. This works; it matches the letters exactly, which makes the story a tempting one to believe. If this is true, we are fortunate—we could be drinking "A Epic Slop" or "Ape Clipso" instead.

The first Pepsi truck. *Courtesy of Pepsi-Cola Bottling Company, New Bern.*

Pepsi is a little newer than its competitive cousin, Coca-Cola—another Southern-bred soft drink that was developed by druggist John Pemberton in Atlanta; and yes, his drink contained cocaine.

Mr. Bradham was fairly quick to enlarge his drink business—by 1903 he was giving it his full attention, moving to a rented warehouse where, in its first year, he sold nearly eight thousand gallons of the syrup. The following year he bought the Bishop Factory and continued to increase his sales.

In 1906 the government passed the Pure Food and Drug Act, which banned a number of strange substances from food, including lead, arsenic, barium and uranium. Pepsi die-hards will be proud to know that Mr. Bradham's soft drink was about the only one that didn't have to change its formula as a result.

The town was proud of Mr. Bradham and his work. A souvenir publication celebrating the bicentennial in 1910 stated, "Pepsi-Cola is New Bern's most valuable invention; it is North Carolina's pride; it is the people's purest drink and is the only manufacturing industry of its kind in the United States."

Bradham's business grew rapidly, but World War I did him in: gambling that sugar prices would go through the roof, he bought huge amounts of sugar. Instead, the prices fell through the basement. Stuck with a huge inventory of overpriced sugar, he was forced into bankruptcy and the business was sold to Craven Holding Corporation in 1920. Shortly after, it was sold to a Wall Street broker. The company changed hands several times and faced at least one more bankruptcy before it settled into its current incarnation as Pepsico.

Mr. Bradham passed from this world in 1934, just a couple of years after the building that housed his historic drink's birthplace. That same year, Pepsi was selling at twelve ounces for a nickel ("Pepsi-Cola hits the spot, For just a nickel you get a lot," the jingle ran)—its competitors were selling at six ounces for a nickel. Pepsi sales skyrocketed.

Today, Pepsico has $32 billion in revenues and 157,000 employees. It is marketed, of course, worldwide.

It is easy to sit in this little facsimile of Mr. Bradham's original shop and be astounded at the leaps Caleb's little drink has made.

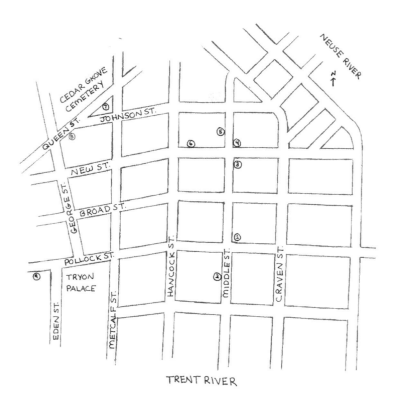

Houses of Worship Tour

The church played an important role in the development of New Bern and North Carolina. Because they were considered a key element of civilization, Baron von Graffenried had carefully placed a site for a church in the center of his town (roughly where Christ Church stands today).

The colony's first ministers were missionaries. The Church of England, through its Society for the Propagation of the Gospel, sent emissaries, including the Reverend James Reed, the highly influential rector of Christ Church who was also the key person behind the founding of the New Bern Academy—the first public school in North Carolina.

Religious persecution was not unknown. In 1741 a group of Baptists were whipped and jailed for asking to build a house of worship. Until the rewriting of the state's constitution in 1835, Catholics could not technically hold a political office. However, as a rule, North Carolina has always been known for its tolerance of "dissenting" faiths.

While the Church of England was the *official* church, it never really enjoyed the power in North Carolina that it did in other colonies.

This fountain greets visitors to a little garden in the Baptist church complex.

A nineteenth-century drawing of First Presbyterian. *Courtesy Tryon Palace Historic Sites and Gardens.*

Left: A chandelier in B'Nai Sholem synagogue.

Below: One of Centenary United Methodist's many towers.

Above: Nineteenth-century baptismal font at Christ Episcopal Church.

Right: Detail of St. Peter's AME Zion.

The interior of the old St. Paul's Roman Catholic Church.

The Moravians had a strong community in central North Carolina, and Presbyterians were a particularly powerful force—especially in the west. In New Bern, in the last quarter of the eighteenth century, the Methodists established a church and not long behind them were the Presbyterians and Baptists. Baptist missionaries were preaching here as early as 1755. Later in the nineteenth century the first Catholic congregation in the state was started; then, about the turn of the century, the first North Carolinian Christian Science church came to be. An important synagogue was also constructed in 1894.

Hope Chapel, housed in a turn-of-the-century doctor's office on Queen Street, is one of the smallest church buildings in New Bern.

African American worshippers were meeting together before the Civil War. One such congregation met at St. Andrew's Methodist and, during the war, became the first African Methodist Episcopal congregation in the South.

Many of the churches we will visit are open for regular tours. All are rightfully proud of their historic heritage and many may be pleased to help you have a look inside or discuss their history with you. It is wise to call the churches in advance as a matter of politeness, or to check in with their administrative offices before you wander the sanctuaries, however—and do be careful to respect these buildings. Observe the altar areas, but do not intrude on them.

Begin by parking on Eden Street, beside the Tryon Palace complex. Walk up to Pollock Street and pay particular attention to the two houses on your left—Hay House and Jones House. Both were owned by founders of the First Presbyterian Church in 1817: carriage maker John Hay and turpentine distiller John Jones. Also note, across the wall into the palace grounds, the large brick stable. In the late nineteenth century this served as a mission chapel for Christ Church.

Turn right and walk three blocks to Middle Street. From this intersection you can look cattycorner across the street and see our first church—indeed, New Bern's first congregation—Christ Episcopal Church.

1. Christ Church
320 Pollock Street
Founded 1715. Current building 1875.

Along Middle Street, very near the intersection of Pollock Street, you will find a wrought-iron gate and, just inside, a charming outdoor chapel. Pick a bench and sit down: you are seated in New Bern's oldest house of worship. The walls are gone and the belfry from which the bell called the faithful is a memory. A grand old cedar tree will serve both as roof and rector; its straddling boughs as ample rafters while that tree's hoary age and ascetic silence, draped in vestments of Spanish moss, will minister to your needs.

Now close your eyes and hear the past: look upon old Governor Dobbs sitting, death etched on his wrinkled brow, his gnarled hand enclosed in the childlike grasp of his sixteen-year-old bride. Hear the whispered words exchanged by Governor William Tryon and his fascinating wife, Margaret, while their four-year-old daughter leafs distractedly through the pages of her prayer book. Hear the soft and loving call of James Reed, one of New Bern's greatest men, as he leads communion, raising the beautiful silver chalice, a gift of King George II. Hear the excited, fervent prayers and pleas of the great eighteenth-century evangelist, George Whitfield. God is in this place, he insists: His love is shining down.

Lean forward now, and a shifting of years will bring to your ear the patriotic shouts of men declaring against George III. That brush of wind may be the dignified visit of another George—Washington, who refused to become an American king. And the sighing sound? Perhaps it is the tears of husbands, wives, fathers and mothers burying their loved ones, laid low by yellow fever at the close of the eighteenth century.

Now return to the mundane present. Squirrels lace their way like little acrobats along the iron fence and children laugh at the playground across the grounds. *Now* you are ready to begin your walking tour.

Christ Church is the epicenter of New Bern's colonial history. The parish (1715) is nearly as old as the town (1710), and stands on the ground specifically laid out for it by founder Christopher von Graffenried ("I divided the village like a cross and in the middle I intended the church," he wrote). For its first thirty-five years it was a house church, until a brick building was constructed in 1750 at the spot on which you now stand. The

Christ Church Destroyed by Fire in 1871

Courtesy of the New Bern Historical Society.

"walls" around you rise from the church's original foundations and give a useful outline of the building's design. Reading the historical markers about the chapel will further fill you in on its history.

By 1820 the congregation was beginning to feel cramped, and so a new building was planned, completed in 1824. Stephen F. Miller, in his *Recollections of New Bern Fifty Years Ago*, recalled watching as local brick mason Bennet Flanner flitted about the uncompleted building like a sailor on rigging:

> *He was bold, fearless and persevering. He moved on the scaffolding high in the air, apparently with as much indifference as if standing on the pavement below. I saw him stand erect nearly half an hour on the apex of the steeple, not less than 150 feet high, with no other surface of support than the twenty or thirty inches diameter on which his feet rested.*

It is a simple matter to gaze at the steeple today and imagine such showmanship.

But Mr. Flanner's steeple would meet a dramatic end. In 1871 Hahn's Bakery stood across the street from the church, where Baxter's Jewelry stands today. On a Tuesday night, January 10, 1871, fire broke out, spreading to buildings on either side. Sparks ignited the church's roof and soon Christ Church was a conflagration of its own. "When the steeple was burning, the large bell gave way and crashed to the ground," historian Gertrude S. Carraway wrote in *Crown of Life*. "Eye witnesses asserted that it tolled mournfully as it fell." By morning the church had been gutted. Only a portion of its original walls remained.

Congregations excel in adversity, and every church seems to have some tale confirming Isaiah's dictum that "a little child will lead them." "A three-year-old child," Ms. Carraway wrote, "watched the fire and remarked to her mother, 'Mama, I've dot free cents, and I'm going to dive it to you to buy some nails to build a new church.'"

The congregation moved temporarily to First Presbyterian while it feverishly raised funds for its razed building. Young girls were among the most heroic, making lamplighters, knitted clothes

Fine woodwork on the balcony rail is accentuated by stained glass.

and quilt squares to raise money for an altar window portraying Jesus blessing little children. Incorporating usable remains of the original structure, the "new" building was finally consecrated on May 23, 1875.

If you make your visit early in the day, you may be pleased to take a free tour of the sanctuary with a knowledgeable and helpful volunteer guide. Within, you can admire the fine Gothic arches and "Turtle Back" ceiling above, and the beautiful stained glass and magnificent pipe organ that spreads across its south balcony's wall. Walnut abounds; a small nineteenth-century marble baptismal font, more noticeable by its fine simplicity, draws your attention as well.

Kept carefully on display behind glass, you can view one of Christ Parish's finest antiquities: a silver communion set (still used), Bible and Book of Common Prayer, all presented to the church by King George II in 1752. The communion service consists of a chalice, paten, two flagons and a basin, each with the Royal Arms of Great Britain stamped on them. The Bible was printed in 1717 and is made the more valuable by a rare misprint—the heading in chapter twenty speaks of the "Parable of the Vinegar" instead of the "Parable of the Vineyard."

A gift upon completion of the first church, this set carries with it a long and curious history. A story, well documented, tells how the service was kept from disappearing into Union hands during the Civil War. The church's rector at the time of the city's fall was Alfred A. Watson. One step ahead of the Yankees, he whisked the service away to Wilmington, where it remained safe for some time. Later during the war it was moved again, this time to Fayetteville, where it was placed in a burlap bag and stuffed into a closet full of rubbish. Union soldiers searched the place for booty, but overlooked the humble sack.

While other churches became hospitals or commissaries during the war, Christ Church was fortunate enough to remain a house of worship, though it was "occupied" by a Union chaplain.

For many years, Christ Church was also the city's primary cemetery (until the yellow fever epidemic of the 1790s filled it up). Many markers are still visible today, giving the church grounds much of their historic air. Among the graves are those of John Wright Stanly and his wife, Ann Cogdell. Stanly was a privateer and revolutionary leader whose wealth helped finance General Nathanael Greene's troops. James Reed, missionary from the Society for the Propagation of the Gospel in Foreign Parts, is also buried here (look along the fence near the northern Middle Street entrance). As a thankful nod to Reverend Reed's efforts in founding North Carolina's first public school, a fine little park and fountain were built in his name across from the church's Pollock Street entrance.

Because of its important place in New Bern's history, you can easily find pamphlets and books to add to your knowledge of Christ Church's past—most are available at the church; you may purchase them when you tour. You can even purchase the church's best-selling cookbook (100,000 copies and growing).

From Christ Episcopal Church you will walk back to Middle Street and turn left. From the corner you can already see the next church, First Baptist.

2. First Baptist
239 Middle Street
Founded 1809. Current building 1847.

First Baptist Church is one of the grand old congregations of New Bern. It was founded in the home of Elijah Clark, at the corner of Middle and Craven Streets, on May 11, 1809, by himself and fellow hopefuls John Brinson and Mary Willis Mitchell. Clark was a carriage maker in the early century (he would go on to become

mayor and sheriff as well) who owned a storehouse and waterfront property that became known as "Baptism shores" for the obviously implied reason.

This does not make him the first Baptist in town—just the first one to succeed in organizing a church. New Bern had been home to Baptist believers since at least the mid-1700s; Benjamin Miller and Peter Peterson Von Horn, two Baptist missionaries, tramped the boards for a couple of years starting in 1755. While the Baptist faith had its adherents, it wasn't popular, for Baptists rejected the notion of infant baptism, and that was counter to the established church of that day. In 1741, fifteen years before Miller and Von Horn preached, a number of Baptist settlers asked the general assembly to allow them to raise a church. The assembly raised a fuss, declaring it would not be

The original Baptist church.

allowed. In case the petitioners didn't understand the meaning of the word "no," they were then publicly whipped and jailed.

For a year or two the Baptists met in Mr. Clark's home. By 1812, however, a wood-box church had been raised at the corner of Johnson and Metcalf Streets—now the site of St. Cyprian's Episcopal Church. If we believe one poetic wag of 1818, it could not have been a comfortable place:

> *The Baptist Barn comes next to view,*
> *Where winter winds turn noses blue,*
> *And shiv'ring devotees retire*
> *Right glad from worship to the fire.*

A uniqueness of this early church was its music program. While other churches steamed away on organs and pianos, First Baptist boasted a glasspiel (similar to Benjamin Franklin's glass harmonica), sometimes accompanied by a violin and cello. The glasspiel is an instrument made up of "hemispherical glasses" (goblets or bowls) "played by touching the edges with dampened fingers," according to the First Baptist website. This old instrument, donated in 1811, is still in the church's possession.

By 1845—whether from blue noses or growing numbers—the Baptists decided it was time for a new home. Property was acquired at its present address and men—one source says Elijah Clark while another cites his grandson, the future Colonel John D. Whitford (perhaps it was both)—traveled to New York to find a design that would meet their needs.

There, the Madison Avenue Baptist Church was just forming in Manhattan. Apparently the New Bern gentlemen saw their plans for a Gothic Revival building, had them modified a bit and came back

home. Carpenter Hardy B. Lane and others were contracted for the work and the church was completed by 1848 for a price of $12,000 (which today would not pay for the parking lot).

Colonel Whitford, who at the turn of the twentieth century laid out a rambling and curious history of our town in *The Home Story of the Walking Stick*, shared his curmudgeonly memories of Baptist services in his day. His complaints are striking in their similarity to those uttered in more modern times.

> *It was then, and in some degree it is yet, an evil which imperiously requires correction, the interruption of public worship by the noise of children, thus converting the church into a nursery. And in this day "late comers," perhaps, are a greater nuisance—much greater, than children…It is, if reprehensible, a pretty picture as she trips gracefully along the aisle, nearly filling it with the feathers and flowers and ribbons shaking on her hat, so jauntily fixed over her smiling or frowning face. Then, too, it gives the other sisters already there something to praise or condemn as to her taste in dressing, when they get home.*

While Reverend Watson was spiriting the Episcopalians' communion service out of town in 1862, the Union boys were converting First Baptist into a center for commissary stores. Her bells rang not to alert worshippers and angels but to tell men in blue it was time to change the guard.

First Baptist enjoyed a celebrity guest during its centennial celebration on November 8, 1948, when President Harry S. Truman, a friend of the pastor, elected to attend service on his way south to a Florida fishing vacation. It must have been an exciting visit, for Truman was riding high on his reelection as U.S. president six days before—one of the tightest races in American history. His opponent, Republican Thomas E. Dewey, had been leading in the polls on election eve.

First Baptist is sometimes called the "Education Church," as four of its former pastors established three major colleges, including Furman College in South Carolina and Meredith College in Raleigh.

The original building peeks out from an amalgam of more modern additions. It is easy enough to imagine the church when the oil was new on its hinges and the squeaking clatter of carriages replaced our modern hum and rumble of cars. Additions (including a garden and fountain) have only added to its charm: a cast-iron fence was wrapped around the church in 1892, and stained glass replaced its clear windows during renovations in 1900. A rose window was added over the balcony in 1943 and a baptistery in 1985.

Back on Middle Street, turn north, passing Christ Episcopal. You will cross Broad Street. Note on your right the First Church of Christ, Scientist. We will not tarry here, but it might be interesting to take a couple of quick notes.

This structure, in Classical Revival, was built in 1907 and designed by Herbert Woodley Simpson—an architect of whom we have heard much in the "Gilded Age—and Beyond" tour, and who will turn up again. This is the first Christian Science church in North Carolina, founded by New Bern native Mary Hatch Harrison after she experienced what she believed to be a faith healing in Boston in 1894. She officially organized the church in 1902. Mary Baker Eddy, the religion's founder, paid a visit in 1904.

Continue to the end of the block where you will come, on your right, upon our next church.

3. Centenary United Methodist
309 New Street (corner of New and Middle)
Founded 1772. Current building 1904.

You could call this the Christmas church. Centenary traces its roots to Christmas 1772. On that day, John Wesley addressed New Bern. Well, he addressed New Bern by proxy.

Joseph Pilmore was a thirty-three-year-old follower of Wesley's who had volunteered to be his American voice. Reverend Pilmore developed the young denomination, especially in New York and Philadelphia. In between his Brotherly Love and Dutchtown jaunts he made Southern tours to establish other churches—much to the chagrin of Reverend James Reed, the Anglican minister at Christ Church, who had a decided distrust of Methodism and its suspected reliance on emotionalism.

These were the days of Methodism's "circuit riding preachers" who rode from town to town, performing weddings, services, baptisms and burials as the need arose. Mr. Pilmore was known to carry his personal library about in his saddlebags.

Robert Williams followed him the next year. Other circuit riders also ministered, among them Bishop Francis Asbury, head of the American branch of the Methodists. He preached fourteen times in this city.

With this founding date, Centenary lays claim to being the oldest Methodist congregation south and west of Baltimore. In 1795 the Methodist Society bought land at the corner of Hancock Street and Pleasant Alley, where they built Andrew's Chapel. Its erection in 1802 brought the total number of church buildings in the city to two. A few years later Stephen M. Chester, a local Presbyterian with a penchant for couplets, would note of that building,

> *Next comes a house without a name—*
> *To that of church it has no claim,*
> *And yet the long misshapen pile*
> *Contains a throng 'twixt either aisle,*
> *And in the galleries perch'd above,*
> *To join in prayer and feasts of love;*
> *Its various worshipers can tell*
> *Why they reject a spire or bell.*

This poem offers some legitimacy to the unofficial nickname of such worshippers: "Shouting Methodists."

St. Andrews would quickly grow to become the city's largest congregation. In 1843 a new building went up—appropriately enough—on New Street. At that time the congregation separated along racial lines, black members remaining with St. Andrew's (it would eventually evolve into St. Peter's AME Zion), the white members going to the new building. Finally, in 1904, a little more than one hundred years after the appearance of its first building, the present Centenary Church was built.

Centenary is one of the most eye-catching structures in New Bern, a Romanesque monolith of columns, towers and spires that is no less impressive when one stands inside the airy sanctuary. The building is yellow brick, with granite and limestone trim. One half expects to see men in mail shirts and crossbows peering out of the bell tower and squires by horses in the parking lot, awaiting their lords' return from service.

The elaborate windows alone are worth a visit. Of German stained glass, they display scenes from the life and stories of Christ. These windows were the subjects of an ecumenical event: on September 15, 1936, an early morning fire struck the church, its blaze and heat sending the ceiling crashing to the floor. Catholic nuns were working across New Street at the time and, fearing for the windows, they prayed together for divine protection. The windows were spared, and repairs enough were done in the church to host a statewide conference in November of that same year.

We should give at least a passing nod to Centenary's architect, Herbert Woodley Simpson—he was quite a presence in his day. According to William S. Powell's *Dictionary of North Carolina Biography*, "Simpson is credited with the design of almost every important structure built in New Bern in the first two decades of the twentieth century."

Roof details of Centenary United Methodist.

The Methodists showed Simpson a New Jersey meetinghouse designed by the famous architect Charles Granville Jones, and at their request, he based this church on that design.

From the corner of Middle and New Streets, continue on Middle Street north. You will pass a rectory house immediately followed by our next subject, the old St. Paul's Roman Catholic Church.

4. St. Paul's
504 Middle Street
Founded 1821. Current building 1841.

Here is the church William Gaston built. No, he was not an architect. But he was many other things: a social reformer, a congressman, assemblyman, a hobnobber of great men, the son of a martyred Patriot, a formidable courtroom lawyer and a State Supreme Court judge.

Through his mother's sacrifices, William became the first student to attend Georgetown University, followed by attendance at the New Bern Academy and finally Princeton, where he received his law degree. Along with his friend John Stanly, William became the most prominent and sought-after lawyer in town and soon turned to a life of politics. As a Catholic, this should have been his undoing; the state constitution, prior to 1835, forbade anyone who did not agree with the "protestant religion" to hold any office. Good lawyer that he was, he argued the technicality that he didn't actually *dis*agree with the Protestant stance and then, as a member of the constitutional committee of 1835, saw to it that the anti-Catholic sentiments were struck.

There was no Catholic church in town, though there were certainly Catholics—a seaport town was hardly likely to be void of papist

thought. The first priest to live in North Carolina was New Bern's Father Patrick Cleary, in 1784. Clinging to his mother's skirts, Gaston probably knew him—though not for long. He was only six years old when the priest, ministering to the victims of a yellow fever epidemic, succumbed to the disease and died.

Once Gaston (whose house and office we examine on the "Colonial–Antebellum" tour) was established in the town, he arranged for a priest to begin holding services in his own home. In 1821, the same year that Christ Church was laying the cornerstone for its second house of worship, Gaston welcomed Bishop John England, who had arrived to set up an official congregation. About two dozen Catholics lived in town at the time, including both whites and African Americans. For the first few years they met at William Gaston's house. Reflecting his own love of the common people, these services tended to cross the social spectrum. Stephen W. Miller, who attended a service in 1822, recalled,

St. Paul's interior about 1880. *Courtesy of North Carolina Department of Archives.*

Attracted by a natural curiosity, and yet with motives of entire respect, I was among a number of spectators in the audience assembled at the house of Mr. Gaston on a Sabbath morning in 1822, to witness, for the first time, the form of worship peculiar to the Catholic Church. The priest who officiated was, I think, the Rev. Mr. O'Donoho. Of the twenty persons, or thereabout, who took the consecrated wafer, kneeling, were a number of French, Spanish and Portuguese residents. There was a moral sublimity in the scene when Mr. Gaston partook of the sacrament in the midst of his Catholic brethren of foreign birth and humble pursuits.

Among the worshippers who were likely at that meeting were John Devereux, a founding member and wealthy merchant in town, and co-founder Joseph Tracy, a free man of color.

Later, Miller heard the bishop speak "in the gorgeous canonicals of his office. He was very logical and eloquent." Bishop England used whatever halls were available to hold his Masses, and it speaks well of the community that the Episcopal and Presbyterian churches were both open to him, as were the academy, the courthouse and the Masonic Lodge.

In 1841, during his last visit to New Bern, Bishop England laid the cornerstone for a new church. The lot had been purchased in readiness back in 1824, but the Catholics' numbers had not been large enough to support its construction before.

Hardy B. Lane, a well-known architect, was hired to raise the building, which Bishop England had proposed to be built of wood, fifty-two feet by thirty-six feet. Humble and lacking even a steeple, it was completed at a cost of under $4,000. The bishop died before its completion in 1841, and St. Paul's had to await the first visit of his successor to be blessed in 1844.

This William Joseph Williams portrait hangs prominently in old St. Paul's.

In 1887 the church became segregated as a new mission was opened for black Catholics at St. Joseph's in town. It would remain so divided until 1965, when the parishes were again united in the midst of the civil rights movement. St. Joseph's now stands as a workshop and storage facility for Tryon Palace Historic Sites and Gardens.

Herbert Woodley Simpson was hired in 1896 to add a central entrance tower and steeple in a simple but graceful Greek Revival style. Although it had gotten along without a pediment for fifty-odd years, it is hard now to picture the church without it.

St. Paul's currently has the largest congregation of any church in the New Bern area. Long ago it outgrew this building; a much vaster structure (seating 1,200) and campus now serves the Catholic community at 3005 Country Club Road, although Masses are also held here at the old St. Paul Church.

When taking this tour, you will be wise to call ahead (252) 638-1984 and arrange to visit the sanctuary of this little church to admire the fine 150-plus-year-old painting that hangs on the wall. This portrait of Christ's crucifixion was made by William Joseph Williams, an American painter of some note who lived in New Bern from 1804 until his death in 1823. Williams is best known for his 1793 portrait of George Washington that hangs at the Alexandria, Virginia Masonic Lodge No. 22. St. Paul's painting features Christ on the cross, gazing to heaven as Mary and John, dressed in bright colors despite the somber theme, look sadly on.

The next step on our walk is an easy one: simply cross the street to B'nai Sholem Temple.

5. Temple Chester B'Nai Sholem
505 Middle Street
Founded 1894. Current building 1908.

Temple Chester B'Nai Sholem has a unique history inasmuch as it was probably named for a child. According to an 1893 article from the *New Bern Weekly Journal*,

> *Our Jewish fellow citizens have organized themselves into a religious congregation, elected Rabbi I. Kaiser, formerly of Petersburg, to be in charge, and intend when a suitable site is secured to erect a synagogue. It is to be known in Hebrew as "Chester, Bnay Scholom [sic]," which being interpreted means "Chester, Child of Peace." It is named in honor of Mr.*

Stained glass in B'nai Sholem.

*Chas. Reizenstein's little son Chester, whose innocent questionings of his
mother as to why they did not have a church to go to led to this movement.*

One could hardly have a more beautiful name than "Child of
Peace" for a house of worship.

Jews lived in New Bern well before 1893. There is some evidence,
through a deed, that a Jewish burial ground existed in 1809 near George
and Queen Streets. Stephen W. Miller's memoirs recall "an old German
trader," a Jew, visiting the town in 1822, selling watches and jewelry.
"There was no synagogue in town," Miller wrote, but "probably a
number of Israelites resided in Newbern, engaged in [mercantile]
traffic of some description." Perhaps John T. Mills was one of them: in
1822 he was offering Hebrew lessons. In 1877 the "Hebrews of New
Bern" purchased land beside the National Cemetery to make a Jewish
cemetery. By 1893 when the congregation was formed, there were a
significant number of Jewish merchants in town.

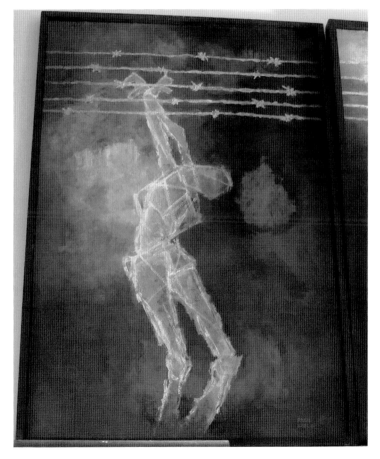

One of Paul Fields's multi-panel Holocaust memorial paintings that hangs in the
synagogue.

B'nai Sholem synagogue.

From 1893 until 1908, when the synagogue was built, the congregation met in various downtown buildings. Once the Jewish community was ready to build its tabernacle, Herbert Woodley Simpson, of course, was hired to design it. He erected a fine neoclassical structure, located almost across the street from two of his previous works, the Catholic St. Paul's (he designed its bell tower, at least) and Centenary Methodist. The portico, with its Corinthian columns and pilasters, quietly recalls the glory of Solomon's temple of old.

In April of 1908 the firm of Rhodes and Underwood set about construction. By the end of the summer it was finished and in use, at a cost of about $5,000. The first service was the wedding of Emma Sultan, held on August 31.

The synagogue was altered somewhat in the 1950s when a kitchen and schoolroom were added at the rear, and new seating was installed for the congregation. A four-panel painting hangs over the east wall, both disturbing and beautiful, honoring the holocaust victims of World War II. It was done by local artist Paul Fields and is on permanent loan. Beneath the panels are lighted memorial boards that list the names of deceased loved ones. But otherwise this house of worship remains much as Mr. Simpson left it.

Walking from B'Nai Sholem, turn south toward the downtown. Looking to your right you will see our next subject, First Presbyterian, a half block down New Street.

6. First Presbyterian
412 New Street
Founded 1817. Current building 1822.

The Episcopalians, Methodists and Baptists were all here first, but the Presbyterians still beat them all out when it comes to having the oldest worship building in town.

Robert Hay was already in his forties when he immigrated to New Bern from Scotland around 1800. A carriage maker with a strong Scottish brogue, he carried Jesus in his heart with a special fervency. It was doubtless one of his greatest disappointments to find that his adopted home had no Calvinist enclave. He turned to the Methodists for worship but could not bring himself to be absorbed into their Armenian ways—even though a pastor called on him to join the congregation from the pulpit.

Hay was not alone in his convictions. Others of note in town bore Calvinist leanings—among them Dr. Benjamin H. Rice, licensed to preach by the Orange Presbytery, Raleigh, in 1810; the wealthy turpentine distiller John Jones; and "Barber John" C. Stanly, mulatto son of John Stanly, the revolutionary Patriot and privateer. Though black and a former slave, Mr. Stanly was by then quite well-to-do with a cadre of slaves of his own.

Slowly, thirteen men and women of like leanings found one another. By 1809 they were holding informal services with Reverend James K. Burch as their newly ordained pastor. Though they would not officially organize for some years, they began laying the groundwork for a church early on: an 1808 article in the *New Bern Herald* advertises a subscription for the purpose of purchasing a lot to erect a "Presbyterian Meeting-House." By 1813 they were sending missions offerings to the Presbytery.

It was the New Bern–born pastor, Reverend John Witherspoon, who finally got the church organized and running. Witherspoon was a man of impeccable breeding—Princeton-educated, the grandson of Princeton president and signer of the Declaration of Independence John Witherspoon. On January 7, 1817, Witherspoon met with Robert Hay, Dr. Hawes and others in the parlor of Mrs. Elizabeth Minor on Craven Street. Naming Hay and Hawes the ruling elders, First Presbyterian officially began with a membership of nine. They worshipped in the old Baptist church.

In 1819 the present lot was purchased at a cost of $1,200. On June 9—a Wednesday—the congregation met briefly at the New Bern Academy, then marched to the lot and laid the cornerstone.

The structure that grew from that lonely stone would be seventy feet by fifty-two, with a seating capacity of eight hundred congregants. We do not know who the architect was, but we know the builders: Uriah Sandy, assisted by Martin Stevenson Sr. and John Dewey (designer and builder of the Masonic Lodge). The church features a broad portico with huge Ionic columns and a four-stage (like inverted nesting blocks) Greek Revival steeple that Sandbeck declares is "the finest of New Bern's many church towers."

It is startling to walk into this building, for the sanctuary faces the opposite way one would expect—with the pulpit toward the front

A raised pulpit is the focus of this airy sanctuary.

entrance. Two rows of large, clear-glass windows bring plenty of light into the sanctuary, which is framed by galleries down either side (in the very old days, this was where the black worshippers sat). On the walls, marble plaques honor the memory of several male and female founders, including Robert Hay and Kitty Green Stanly, a former slave who was the wife of John C. Stanly.

Much of the funding for the church came from the sale of pews—a common practice in those days (Christ Church also raised money this way). They ran from $150 to $350. On January 6, 1822, the church was finished. An additional one-story session house was built in 1858 for $1,500 in Greek Revival style, then was enlarged in the 1880s and picked up and moved from the side of the property to its present location in the middle of the green in 1923. In 1903 a cast-iron fence was added to the grounds.

The Federal Building (old post office) cupola rises as a kind of sibling—church and state—to the Presbyterian steeple.

During the Civil War this congregation, like most in town, was decimated by the flight of New Bern's citizens. The Yankees took over the church and its manse, using it as a hospital and surgeons' quarters. The church pews were spared only when members who had not fled convinced the doctors to place planks over them for beds rather than destroying them. A dead house was built on the grounds while the steeple was used as a lookout station. Soldiers' names are carved into the woodwork there.

When visiting First Presbyterian, it is worth arranging to go inside. A quiet stroll will quickly put you in mind of that founding congregation: you can imagine the preacher speaking from the raised pulpit and hear Mr. Hay uttering his famously long prayers from his pew eight rows back.

Now walk back to Middle Street and turn left. You will cross Johnson Street, passing the library on your left. At the end of the block, on the right-hand side, you will see a fine little gambrel-roofed home that is next on our tour.

7. Elijah Clark House
616 Middle Street
Built circa 1760–80

Elijah Clark's house at the turn of the century. *Courtesy of First Baptist Church.*

We will not spend too much time at this quaint little house, but its role in the founding of the Baptist church in New Bern leaves us obliged to give it a salute.

Elijah Clark—you will remember him as one of three founders of the First Baptist Church—bought the house early in the nineteenth century. Peter Sandbeck suggests a construction date between 1760 and 1780. A historic marker on the building emphatically declares its birth at 1748, a date that is perhaps based on the lot's original purchase in 1746.

It has a gambrel roof, denoting its late eighteenth-century construction. Today it is a private residence, pleasantly decorated with a low picket fence, a simple garden, a larger privacy fence at the back (Craven Street) side and enough angles to keep one studying its fascinating lines for some time.

Elijah Clark was, in his youth, something of a bad boy. His grandson, Colonel John D. Whitford, recalled a humorous story of Elijah's youth when a horse-racing track still stood outside of town:

> *For riding a race there on Sunday, when a boy, Elijah Clark never hesitated to admit he deserved [the] flogging he received from his father for it, whatever the reward from others might have been. Perhaps the horse*

A ceramic boy perpetually gazes at the founding Baptist home from the corner of the Elijah Clark property.

he mounted was not successful. It will be remembered the story of the old Baptist preacher, who after severely reprimanding his son for spiriting off his old mare to race her on Sunday enquired "Who beat."

"Oh I did" replied the son.

"That's right, if you will race beat them if you can" was now the gentle answer.

Along with starting a church in his home, Mr. Clark led an active political life. In the 1830s, the city's magistrates appointed him as sheriff. Eventually, however, this became an elected office. With the whiskey-hued electioneering of that day, this was bad news for devout Elijah. A man could not easily win if he wasn't willing to lubricate the voters with free rounds of rum. Mr. Clark declared he would sooner lose the election than buy it with the devil's brew. He lost—and did so proudly.

Being none too fond of Yankees, he left the town when it fell in the Civil War and died a refugee at Graham in Alamance County three months later in June 1862.

Colonel Whitford and historians at First Baptist all identify this house as the one in which Elijah Clark began his church. The biggest problem with this suggestion is that, according to Sandbeck, Mr. Clark did not buy it until 1812—the same year the first house of worship was finished. It is a conundrum: which to believe? The records put the house's purchase at three years after the congregation's first services, but Mr. Whitford should certainly have known in which building his grandfather started the show.

Whether this *was* the actual house in which those early services took place or not, the importance of Mr. Clark's home is not diminished. He was, as Whitford attested, one who "gave more for the churches than any other citizen…ever did for any church or churches before or since his death in New Bern."

We now take Craven Street where Middle Street merges onto it and follow it north to where it ends on Queen Street. Turn left, passing St. Cyprian's Episcopal (built circa 1910). Cedar Grove Cemetery is on your right. Crossing Johnson Street, you will come upon our next church on your left.

8. St. Peter's AME Zion
617 Queen Street
Founded 1863. Current building 1923–40.

It is a recent structure, this AME Zion house of worship—it was started in 1923 and did not reach its present state until 1940. In a city abounding with hoary walls, St. Peter's seems almost a babe in arms.

But as to its congregation, this is the granddaddy of black churches in New Bern—and the patriarch of AME churches in the South.

St. Peter's was founded by a Civil War missionary from the North, James Walker Hood. He was not your typical American missionary of the day—if for no other reason than he was *African* American.

Hood was born to a free family in southeastern Pennsylvania in 1831. His parents were devout (they'd started a colored Methodist church) and decidedly abolitionist. By age twelve, he was making abolition speeches. In 1860 Hood was ordained a deacon with the AME Zion Church, an all-black denomination founded in 1796. He started his missionary career in Nova Scotia and then was resituated in abolition-soaked Hartford, Connecticut. From here, Reverend Hood heard the mission call to war-torn New Bern, North Carolina.

His arrival was nothing short of an act of courage. Though ringed by forts and brimming with soldiers in blue, New Bern was still open to attack; any black minister daring to preach freedom could well have found himself killed, locked up or enslaved. And, as a coastal town, New Bern was a breeding ground for disease—upon his arrival Reverend Hood immediately caught smallpox (an epidemic that had caused the Union health department to temporarily close most of the city's churches). But above all this, Hood knew the town was full to overflowing with newly freed Negroes—men and women who were mostly uneducated, bewildered by their newfound status and grasping to learn what it meant—a people who, Reverend Hood knew, had many more years of prejudice to overcome, and who were desperate for a spiritual father to show the way.

He found a large body of black worshippers at St. Andrew's Chapel, then a part of the Methodist Episcopal church. The congregants agreed to reorganize under the AME banner and thus the mother church of the African Methodist Episcopal denomination in the South was born. Hood went on to become an influential leader of the black community in North Carolina, and a bishop within the AME denomination.

Later, in 1879, the congregation renamed itself St. Peter's and erected their new structure on this site on Queen Street, facing Cedar Grove Cemetery across the road. A frame church, it was enlarged and re-faced with brick in 1914. A new organ was purchased by 1922—the finest in town, according to some.

Unfortunately, the church met tragedy that same year. On December 1, New Bern experienced the worst fire in its history—an apocalyptic blaze that took out most of the black district. The fire crossed Cedar Grove Cemetery, leaping from tree to tree; it destroyed dozens of homes and businesses while most of the town's firefighters were away watching their sons play a championship football game near Raleigh. In the end, St. Peter's was completely engulfed and destroyed. Joe Gaskill, a church member in those days, later recalled,

It was the finest black church in town and they also had a wonderful organ that they just bought for three thousand dollars. No other church in town had one like that. And then when they had to rebuild it, the black folks literally built it brick by brick. I remember sometimes the vegetable women would say if they sold you vegetables, "Give me a quarter for my church." They really worked hard, and it was finished and used I believe for the first time Easter 1940.

He added:

Our church, St. Peter's AME Zion Church was completely destroyed by fire as we hosted the fifty-nine sessions of the North Carolina Conference. The Bishop, Ministers, delegates, parishioners, had to flee for their safety. In as much as we had a large congregation, the city of New Bern personnel allowed us to use West Street School auditorium for our worship services. The Bishop appointed my grandfather, the Rev. William Martin, to be the shepherd of the flock. In the meantime, the sites were being cleared and the present basement was being laid. In 1923 we were able to go back on Queen Street.

The church you see now is the result of that effort. It is Gothic Revival, complete with buttresses and lancet-arched windows. The sanctuary is vaulted, with a series of receding arches making up the altar area.

In the narthex, the congregation proudly displays photographs of the burned-out first St. Peter's and of its founder, Bishop James Hood.

New Bern has a wealth of historic black churches. Six are listed on the National Register of Historic Places: St. Peter's, St. Cyprian's

The ruins of the old church after the 1922 fire, in a photo by Bayard Wootten. *Courtesy of New Bern Fireman's Museum.*

Episcopal Church, Ebenezer Presbyterian Church, Rue Chapel AME Church, St. John's Missionary Baptist Church and First Missionary Baptist Church.

From here, follow Queen Street to the corner at George Street, turning left. Walk three blocks to Pollock Street (you will find yourself facing the front gates of Tryon Palace) and turn right. You will cross Eden Street and, about halfway down this block, find yourself across the street from our final destination.

9. All Saints Chapel
809 Pollock Street
Built 1895. Deconsecrated 1938.

In a way, we have come full circle. This last church is also our first—inasmuch as it was built as an extension of Christ Church's ministry to the community.

This little Gothic Revival house of worship almost begs to have a background of scenic hills behind it, perhaps with Heidi, and some goats nibbling on mountain flowers off to one side. Instead, it is surrounded by private dwellings on considerably flat land. Its worshippers of the past have given way to dragonflies and concrete toads and bunnies—for it has become Late Bloomers Garden and Gift Shop, a charming little store of sculptures, earthy bric-a-brac, thermometers, birdfeeders and birdbaths to decorate a home or yard. But every decoration for sale suits this venerable building's temperament well.

All Saints's history begins at the Tryon Palace stable. There, in one of the town's oldest structures (built 1767–70), Christ Church had been running a mission chapel since the 1860s. Francis F. Duffy wanted the place and bought it in March of 1895 for $1,900, so the parish decided to build its own outreach chapel and school at another spot nearby.

A committee was named and chose this site at 809 Pollock Street. The church already owned the land, and Margaret D. Nelson covered the costs of construction.

The building went up, its design borrowing from both Stick Style and Carpenter Gothic, and was painted brown (as it is today). Inside, the roof is built in exposed "scissors" trusses; this pattern, as noted in Sandbeck's book, is emphasized on the exterior through its belfry trim.

By 1909 a schoolhouse was erected behind the building for underprivileged children. Use of the church as a house of worship declined over the years; in 1938 it was officially deconsecrated by Bishop Thomas C. Darst. For a time after, the church was used as a nursery school.

Eventually the New Bern Historical Society took over the building, restoring it in the 1980s and selling it to its current owners. You can do worse than to end a walking tour by shopping in one of this town's most attractive shops!

When you have finished your time at All Saints Chapel, continue your walk down Pollock Street toward the river. In a very short time you will find yourself at the corner of Eden Street, where you first began.

Downtown New Bern has plenty of good eating.

A romantic horse and carriage ride is one good way to tour historic homes around downtown New Bern. The carriage runs every day but Sunday.

Also from The History Press

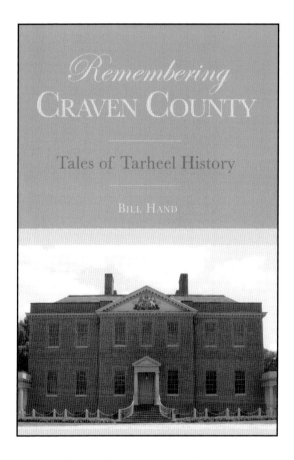

Remembering Craven County
Tales of Tarheel History
Bill Hand
978-1-59629-157-7 • 128 pp. • $19.99

Situated in the heart of eastern North Carolina, Craven County—
New Bern in particular—has as much rich history as quaint charm.
With a keen eye and clever style, Bill Hand takes readers on a romp
through Craven County's history and paints a fascinating picture
of the area's past.

Visit us at

www.historypress.net